The Reference Shelf™

Homeland Security

Edited by Norris Smith and Lynn M. Messina

The Reference Shelf
Volume 76 • Number 1

The H. W. Wilson Company
2004

The Reference Shelf

The books in this series contain reprints of articles, excerpts from books, addresses on current issues, and studies of social trends in the United States and other countries. There are six separately bound numbers in each volume, all of which are usually published in the same calendar year. Numbers one through five are each devoted to a single subject, providing background information and discussion from various points of view and concluding with a subject index and comprehensive bibliography that lists books, pamphlets, and abstracts of additional articles on the subject. The final number of each volume is a collection of recent speeches, and it contains a cumulative speaker index. Books in the series may be purchased individually or on subscription.

Library of Congress has cataloged this title as follows:

Homeland security / edited by Norris Smith and Lynn M. Messina.
     p.cm. — (The reference shelf ; v. 76, no. 1)
     Includes bibliographical references and index.
     ISBN 0-8242-1033-6 (alk. paper)
     1. Terrorism—United States—Prevention. 2. National security—United States.
     3. Emergency management—United States. I. Smith, Norris. II. Messina, Lynn
M. III. Series.

HV6432 .H657 2004
363.32'0973—dc22

2003070366

Cover: Logan International Airport in Boston, Ma., November 28, 2001. (AP Photo/Michael Dwyer)

Visit H.W. Wilson's Web site: www.hwwilson.com

Printed in the United States of America

Contents

Preface

This book is a compendium of articles about American efforts to achieve homeland security in the wake of 9/11. The atrocities of that day put an end to any notions of invulnerability in the United States and left the nation with a double domestic agenda: trying to anticipate and prevent another attack and bracing to meet one, should it occur. No one familiar with the United States would consider these missions easy. The country is huge, stretching across an entire continent and beyond, and generally prosperous, presenting an array of possible targets; it is an open society and a magnet for immigrants; its economy depends on commerce, much of which is international; borders are lightly guarded; immigration laws are not consistently enforced; government can be inefficient, with overlapping jurisdictions and competing interests; and the citizenry, though resourceful, is not particularly amenable to organization.

Americans are no strangers to disaster—earthquakes, fires, storms, and floods have in fact provided a template for emergency response. And terrorist actions themselves are not unknown in the United States, although they are usually home-grown, rather than foreign-sponsored, and limited in their lethal scope. The 1995 Oklahoma City bombing was the first large-scale terrorist action on U.S. soil; the 9/11 attacks introduced the new twist of suicide bombers and forced a massive reassessment of the nation's vulnerability.

By executive order, President George W. Bush established the Office of Homeland Security on October 8, 2001, with Tom Ridge, a former governor of Pennsylvania, as director. Although Bush at first resisted proposals for a cabinet-level department to meet the threat of terrorism, on November 25, 2002, he signed a bill creating the Department of Homeland Security. Ridge was sworn in as secretary the following January.

The new department is largely a reorganization of existing government agencies in the light of present-day dangers. Twenty-two agencies that used to be independent, or attached to other cabinet departments, have been moved into Homeland Security and sometimes altered in the process, so that roles would not be duplicated. The department has only just begun to function, and its record cannot yet be appraised. However, it has achieved some success in rationalizing the bureaucratic maze, carrying out a long-overdue reform of the Immigration and Naturalization Service, and beefing up the Coast Guard and the Border Patrol. The major intelligence services remain outside the department's purview, however, and within the department there is confusion as to accountability and enforcement, and an apparent hesitancy about taking the lead in setting priorities. The department's attempts to warn of impending danger through a color-coded alert system, and to encourage citizens to undertake their own defense with duct tape and plastic sheeting, have excited both alarm and derision and fueled suspicions that the terrorist threat is sometimes manipulated for political ends. However, even if the department has occasionally cried wolf, real wolves are out there, bigger and badder than the villains of storybooks, and no one is likely to forget it.

This book is divided into six sections. The first presents an overview of the tasks faced by the department and of the uneven progress that has been made in the past two years. Despite considerable improvement, great areas of vulnerability persist, and some experts feel that another successful attack—probably a suicide mission—is likely. Part II focuses on local security and "first responders"—the police, fire, and medical personnel who are now attempting to prepare for a disaster of unknown nature and proportions. Part III is concerned with U.S. intelligence services, their conflicts and weaknesses, and their newly expanded powers of investigation, while Part IV deals with immigration and border controls. Airline safety and seaport security are the subjects of Part V; other possible targets and other modes of attack—nuclear, cyber, and biological—are briefly surveyed in Part VI.

Certain themes reappear throughout the book. One is money. With two overseas military occupations in progress, a sputtering domestic economy, and a diminished tax base, the United States will be hard put to pay for advanced security projects that could require years of research and development. Even basic measures like hiring additional border guards can be expensive. The reader will encounter many complaints about shortfalls in the funds available for homeland security, and no very reliable assurances of monies to come. A second recurring theme is technology. High-tech solutions to many of the problems of surveillance and response are quite possible—some are on the drawing boards and several are already on the market. However, experts are unanimous in cautioning that technology is only as good as the people who maintain and use it. Screens have to be watched, data must be analyzed, and decisions have to be made, sometimes in a split second, by fallible human beings. Perhaps the deepest doubts about advanced technology, though, relate to privacy and civil liberties—the third recurring theme. Civil liberties are often overlooked in wartime, when victory becomes all-important. A swirl of controversy surrounds the PATRIOT Act, which has expanded the government's powers of investigation and detention, some say too far. In the end the American people will have to decide where the balance between security and freedom should lie.

Homeland security is still very much a work in progress. By the time this book goes to press, some of the deficiencies described in these articles may already be under repair, or new problems may have emerged. We have tried, however, to choose articles that are current and will not date quickly but remain pertinent and interesting to the general reader. We would like to thank the authors and the original publishers for permission to reprint, and Richard Stein, Jennifer Peloso, and the indefatigible Sandra Watson for their help in producing this book.

Norris Smith
Lynn M. Messina
February 2004

I. Overview of Homeland Security

Editors' Introduction

T his chapter presents an overview of homeland security in the United States. The writers whose articles are reprinted here address the various ways in which the Department of Homeland Security and other government agencies—federal, state, and local—are working to prevent another attack like that which occurred on September 11, 2001, even as they plan for that possibility. As the articles illustrate, that dual task presents an enormous challenge to the new department, one that many safety experts wonder if it can meet as it continues to shape its policies and procedures. Several of the department's concerns introduced here—such as those dealing with nuclear, chemical, and biological attacks, as well as the readiness of police, fire, and medical personnel (so-called "first responders") and the tracking of immigrants—are covered in greater depth elsewhere in this book, as is the challenge to civil liberties posed by many homeland security measures.

The chapter opens with two articles published on the second anniversary of the 9/11 attacks. "How Safe Are You?" from the *Fort Worth Star-Telegram* assesses the progress made in homeland security over the past two years and identifies some continuing weaknesses, particularly in public health, the flow of intelligence, and the funding and organization of "first responders." These complaints, along with concerns over the safety of America's chemical plants, are echoed in Muriel Dobbin's "Amid Safeguards, Threat Remains," published in the *Sacramento Bee*. Dobbin details the findings of the House Select Committee on Homeland Security, but she focuses first on the public's perception of threat, which she describes as increasingly relaxed—perhaps too relaxed, considering the dangers that persist. Most Americans were horrified by 9/11 without being directly affected by it, she says, and although they now recognize the possibility of another attack, it still seems remote from daily life.

In "Homeland Insecurity," reprinted from *Popular Science*, Merrell Noden describes his stroll through New York City with a security expert who, a year after 9/11, identifies the particular vulnerabilities of urban environments, right down to the trash cans. Better equipment and technology, Noden believes, could improve security greatly, but a fundamental shift in thinking will also be necessary, if we are to grapple with these problems successfully.

The cargo inspectors, immigration agents, and epidemiologists that Shane Harris discusses in "Detecting the Threat: Technology and the War on Terror," from *Government Executive*, have made that shift in thinking: They are fully aware of a possible disaster and absolutely determined to prevent it. Harris reports on an astonishing range of technologies that are now being used to make the nation safer—or (more often) that are desperately needed for that effort. In time, Harris hopes, science, sophisticated technology, and alert, knowledgeable people will combine to "even the odds" against terror, but he does not expect that to happen very soon. He adds that there are promising nonemergency applications to some of the new programs and inventions, which may benefit society in the future.

Finally, in "The General Nobody Knows," originally published in *Newsweek*, Michael Hirsh introduces General Ed Eberhart, head of the Northern Command (NORTHCOM), a newly established military command for the North American continent. The continental United States has not been a theater of war since the 19th century, but in the Pentagon's view, it is now. General Eberhart's forces are there to intercept attacks, defend the home ground, and provide backup for civilian agencies and "first responders," as authorized. There is some uneasy sense that the army's presence here today could violate the Posse Comitatus Act, forbidding the government from using the military for direct domestic law enforcement. General Eberhart, who is keenly aware of this concern, is keeping a reassuringly low profile as he develops liaisons with the many agencies that might one day need his help. Since he has access to Defense intelligence, he can also provide prompt and relatively specific information about terrorist threats to those who need to know.

The chapter also contains sidebars, including a flowchart showing the basic structure of the new Department of Homeland Security (into which 22 agencies have now been folded) and the department's own color-coded alert system indicating the current level of threat and prescribing appropriate actions. (The announced threat level applies to the United States as a whole; certain areas, such as Washington, D.C., and New York City, are always one notch higher.) The warning system was introduced in the spring of 2002 at the "yellow" or "significant" level, which is as low as it has ever gone. It has been raised to "orange" or "high" five times, most recently in December 2003 in response to rumors of an air attack.

How Safe Are You?[1]

FORT WORTH STAR-TELEGRAM, SEPTEMBER 11, 2003

Do Americans feel safer today than they did two years ago, in the stupefying hours and days that followed the Sept. 11 attacks on the World Trade Center and Pentagon and the crash of an airliner in a Pennsylvania field?

The news leading up to today's observance of those sobering events has been sprinkled with survey information about Americans' perceptions of safety.

Nearly three-fourths of Americans expect occasional ongoing terrorist acts in the United States, and 58 percent worry that another attack will soon hit the nation, according to a poll released Sept. 4 by the Washington, D.C.–based Pew Research Center for the People and the Press.

Yet the same survey has 75 percent of the respondents saying the U.S. government is doing a good job in reducing terror threats.

Just how good a job is the government doing?

The report card is mixed.

Securing air travel topped lawmakers' post-9/11 "will do" list. The nation's leadership is historically good at retroactively preparing for the most recent emergency.

Baggage and body screening, restrictions for carry-on items, air marshals, armed pilots on the flight deck—all of these tangible measures add to the flying public's sense of security and were crucial in the days following Sept. 11.

But has too much focus been put on commercial airlines to the detriment of rail or cargo transportation?

This week's case of a man shipping himself from New Jersey to Texas raises questions about the security of America's cargo operations and should prompt Congress and the Department of Homeland Security to revisit priorities.

Will a future target for terrorists be at an airport, or will it be the disruption of the nation's economic and social infrastructure—ground transportation, the electrical grid, water purification and distribution systems, financial and banking systems, and telecommunications?

It is clear from the congressional investigations that deconstructed the events leading to Sept. 11 that communication—or lack of effective communication—among government agencies may have contributed to America's vulnerability. "Connecting the dots"

---

1. Article from *Fort Worth Star-Telegram* September 11, 2003. Copyright © *Fort Worth Star-Telegram*. Reprinted with permission.

wasn't happening, and Congress moved quickly in passing the USA PATRIOT Act to lower the walls that blocked the sharing of information among federal law enforcement agencies.

Yet a General Accounting Office report released this month indicates that communication from the federal level to state and local governments is still lacking.

"No level of government perceived the process as effective, particularly when sharing information with federal agencies," the GAO report said. "Information on threats, methods and techniques of terrorists is not routinely shared; and the information that is shared is not perceived as timely, accurate or relevant."

The GAO survey revealed that officials at all levels were dissatisfied with the intelligence they are receiving. Almost every city surveyed said that officials needed information on the movement of known terrorists, but only 15 percent of respondents said that they received this intelligence.

Information isn't all that cities need. Funds to shore up training and equipment for first responders is in short supply. As much as it

---

The Department of Homeland Security has allocated $4.4 billion to states and municipalities for enhanced protections.

---

may appear that federal lawmakers have a money tree planted in the Capitol Rotunda that perpetually drops ripened bills into their outstretched hands, lawmakers have finite financial resources to commit to domestic security.

The Department of Homeland Security has allocated $4.4 billion to states and municipalities for enhanced protections. Another $3.5 billion should be on the way in the next fiscal year. But those dollars come with strings.

Concerned that money would be shifted to fill other budget gaps, the federal government mandates that these grants go to programs directly related to homeland security. That means equipment but not people or infrastructure.

So even though federal dollars may be supplementing local coffers, many states and cities have new equipment but no personnel to use it.

"Without question, the single largest challenge is that we are unable to really hire people to support a lot of the federal equipment we're being asked to deploy," said Clifford Ong, director of Indiana's Counter-Terrorism and Security Council, in *Government Executive* magazine. "That is an intractable problem for us."

How that money is allocated is also a problem. This month, members of the Senate Judiciary subcommittee on technology, terrorism and homeland security criticized the Homeland Security Department's inadequate and archaic funding formulas, saying that the money should be distributed based on risks to communities and not as equitable percentages.

Of course, average Americans don't give a fig about federal funding formulas. They want to know if their local hospitals will be prepared to handle a sudden surge in patients should there be a bioterrorist attack.

The average American won't like the answer to that question.

In an August report from the GAO, most of the country's urban hospitals said they do not have sufficient resources to handle such an event.

More than 80 percent of the hospitals surveyed said they have developed emergency response plans for bioterrorism, but most of the 2,041 urban hospitals also reported that they lacked enough medical equipment to treat large numbers of victims of a sudden terrorist attack.

And how goes the initiative to prepare the country for a potential smallpox attack by vaccinating health care workers and first responders?

Not well. Of the 439,000 individuals who were identified in December 2002 by the Department of Health and Human Services as those to receive inoculation in the first phase, only 36,000 have been vaccinated.

What about border security?

U.S. Sen. John Cornyn toured Texas-Mexico customs operations on Monday before speaking at a border conference in San Antonio.

"I was troubled by what I saw," the junior senator from Texas said. "The sheer number of potential security risks, the horrible costs of human smuggling, and the enormous gap between the resources offered to border agencies and the resources needed to enforce the law are issues that have gone unaddressed by the federal government."

What about the federal government's cyber security? Again, here's what the GAO has to say: "Our most recent analyses of audit and evaluation reports for the 24 major departments and agencies continued to highlight significant information security weaknesses that place a broad array of federal operations and assets at risk of fraud, misuse and disruption," Robert Dacey, director of the GAO information technology team, testified this month before a Senate committee meeting.

In November 2002, retired Brig. Gen. David Grange—a former Delta Force member, Green Beret and Army Ranger—bluntly described the United States as a theater of war with a "truly target-rich environment."

Unfortunately—two years after 9/11—it still is.

Threat Conditions

A tool to combat terrorism. Threat Conditions characterize the risk of terrorist attack. Protective Measures are the steps that will be taken by government and the private sector to reduce vulnerabilities. The HSAS establishes five Threat Conditions with associated suggested Protective Measures:

Low Condition
Green

Low risk of terrorist attacks. The following Protective Measures may be applied:

- Refining and exercising preplanned Protective Measures
- Ensuring personnel receive training on HSAS, departmental, or agency-specific Protective Measures; and
- Regularly assessing facilities for vulnerabilities and taking measures to reduce them.

Guarded Condition
Blue

General risk of terrorist attack. In addition to the previously outlined Protective Measures, the following may be applied:

- Checking communications with designated emergency response or command locations;
- Reviewing and updating emergency response procedures; and
- Providing the public with necessary information.

Elevated Condition
Yellow

Significant risk of terrorist attacks. In addition to the previously outlined Protective Measures, the following may be applied:

- Increasing surveillance of critical locations;
- Coordinating emergency plans with nearby jurisdictions;
- Assessing further refinement of Protective Measures within the context of the current threat information; and
- Implementing, as appropriate, contingency and emergency response plans.

High Condition
Orange

High risk of terrorist attacks. In addition to the previously outlined Protective Measures, the following may be applied:

- Coordinating necessary security efforts with armed forces or law enforcement agencies;
- Taking additional precaution at public events;
- Preparing to work at an alternate site or with a dispersed workforce; and
- Restricting access to essential personnel only.

Severe Condition
Red

Severe risk of terrorist attacks. In addition to the previously outlined Protective Measures, the following may be applied:

- Assigning emergency response personnel and pre-positioning specially trained teams;
- Monitoring, redirecting or constraining transportation systems;
- Closing public and government facilities; and
- Increasing or redirecting personnel to address critical emergency needs.

Source: The White House, *www.whitehouse.gov* March 12, 2002

Amid Safeguards, Threat Remains[2]

BY MURIEL DOBBIN
SACRAMENTO BEE, SEPTEMBER 11, 2003

The day that changed America two years ago bequeathed a legacy of dark memories and a recurrent fear that the worst terrorist strike on the U.S. mainland would not be the last.

On the anniversary of the 9/11 attacks, the nation still struggles with the question of whether actions taken by the government since then have made America safer.

Rep. Christopher Cox, chairman of the House Committee on Homeland Security, has presided over 23 hearings at which he has heard testimony on the progress made in safeguarding the country, as well as charges that Americans remain dangerously unprepared for another attack. There has been significant improvement in national security, from airports to borders, Cox said. But he also acknowledged that the nation must remain on guard.

"There is no question that the United States is safer," Cox, R-Newport Beach, said in a telephone interview. "The country is far better secured than it was in 2001, but it is only a beginning. Much has been done, but there are miles and miles to go. The war on terrorism is the story of the 21st century."

His comments were underscored by a recent report by the London-based World Markets Research Center, which found that the United States ranked fourth in an index assessing the risk in 186 countries of a terrorist attack. The only countries more at risk were Colombia, Israel and Pakistan, the report said.

There are signs that Americans are relaxing, despite government warnings that Osama bin Laden's Al Qaeda network remains a threat.

Surveys showed that over the past two years, the number of those seriously worried about the likelihood of terrorist attacks on American soil dropped from 41 percent to 29 percent, while confidence in the capacity of the government to protect citizens from terrorism remained steady.

Polls by the American Enterprise Institute, a conservative Washington think tank, tracking public reaction over the past two years showed that in summer 2002, 62 percent of respondents said life in America would "never" completely return to the pre-terrorism era.

Yet 73 percent admitted terrorism had not changed their personal lives or activities. After the terrorist threat alert was raised to code orange in February, 90 percent reported they went about life as usual.

And in July, a Pew Research Center survey showed 56 percent thought the government was doing "fairly well" in reducing the terrorism threat.

Cox defended the performance of the Department of Homeland Security, an amalgam of 22 agencies and 122,000 employees, with a reminder that it has not been in existence long. The department has had growing pains, he said, not the least of which was the development of its own internal intelligence service, revised Bureau of Customs and Immigration programs aimed at increased protection of commercial cargo at ports and borders, and a crackdown on potential loopholes for illegal immigrants in the former Immigration and Naturalization Service, now part of Homeland Security.

But over the course of his hearings, Cox heard a continuing flow of criticism and complaints from authorities on counterterrorism,

---

> *"I concede that in some ways we are safer now than we were two years ago, but we are not safe enough."*—Jamie Metzl, Council on Foreign Relations

---

security and health. There were calls for expedited money and training for emergency responders, as well as more focus on public health services unprepared for—and potentially overwhelmed by—a possible bioterrorism attack.

There were lingering grumbles about national security alerts, with the Congressional Research Service urging that in order to avoid unnecessary anxiety, the public should be told more specifically about the nature of a threat before the system is used.

One of the sharpest criticisms of how government has handled the post-9/11 era came in midsummer from an independent task force, sponsored by the New York–based Council on Foreign Relations, that charged the police, fire department and ambulance personnel who bear the brunt of attacks were so underfunded that the currently budgeted $5 billion a year should be increased fivefold.

The impact of the report was increased by the fact that the 20-member panel was headed by former Sen. Warren Rudman of New Hampshire, who was co-author of a pre-9/11 warning of a major attack on America.

"I concede that in some ways we are safer now than we were two years ago, but we are not safe enough," Jamie Metzl, a member of the panel, said in an interview. "We know the terrorists are organizing to get us and we are still very vulnerable."

He cited as examples of vulnerability the failure to establish "national standards of preparedness" that would ensure funding of emergency responders, the continuing need to enhance security at the nation's 15,000 chemical sites in or near urban areas, and the threat of sabotage in container cargo shipped or flown into the United States.

"This is a communications challenge for the administration," said Metzl, who said that both President Bush and Homeland Security Secretary Tom Ridge needed to convey "more sense of urgency" to the public.

Counterterrorism expert Neil Livingstone agreed that the administration had not sold the terrorist threat as strongly as it should have.

He recommended that the color-coded national alert system should be more specifically targeted, and he faulted the government for failing to provide direct federal aid for first responders, to take more steps to harden borders, or to further tighten security at ports and airports.

"We're in something like a faux peace right now."—**Neil Livingstone, counterterrorism expert**

"Overall, it is hit and miss," he said. "The American public is starting to respond with a ho-hum attitude that this will pass. It won't. The threat is still out there, and I don't doubt there will be another major attack. This will go on for years, maybe into decades."

Livingstone suggested that the reason America had not undergone another massive attack might be attributable to the fact that Al Qaeda "was surprised by its own success on 9/11 and wasn't prepared to follow up effectively."

The controversial detention of hundreds of potential terrorism suspects in the days immediately after the attacks on the East Coast "could have gone a long way to dismantle their plans to carry out further attacks," he said.

"We're in something like a faux peace right now," said Livingstone. "We think we have rolled up about 65 percent of the Al Qaeda leadership. What we forget is that a lot of younger terrorists are coming up, and they spend all their time figuring out how to kill Americans."

A warning of the possibility of terrorism overwhelming the public health system was sounded by Shelley Hearne, executive director of the Trust for America's Health, a nonprofit, nonpartisan health advocacy group now preparing a "scorecard" on the need to upgrade state services.

In a report in June, the Trust for America's Health described as "unprepared and overwhelmed" the nation's public health laboratories, which serve as front-line defenders in the case of bioterror attack. Noting that such laboratories were responsible for identifying any biological weapons used in an attack, the report said that despite being overwhelmed by the demands of the anthrax crisis following 9/11, federal support was still lacking.

Cox acknowledged rising concern over possible loss of civil liberties in the drive to root out terrorists.

He cautioned against reactions that would diminish traditions and structure of the United States, noting that the destruction of the U.S. economy and way of life was the terrorist goal.

"We have a free and open society, and we don't have to spend ourselves into bankruptcy or do away with civil liberties in our panic to protect ourselves," he said.

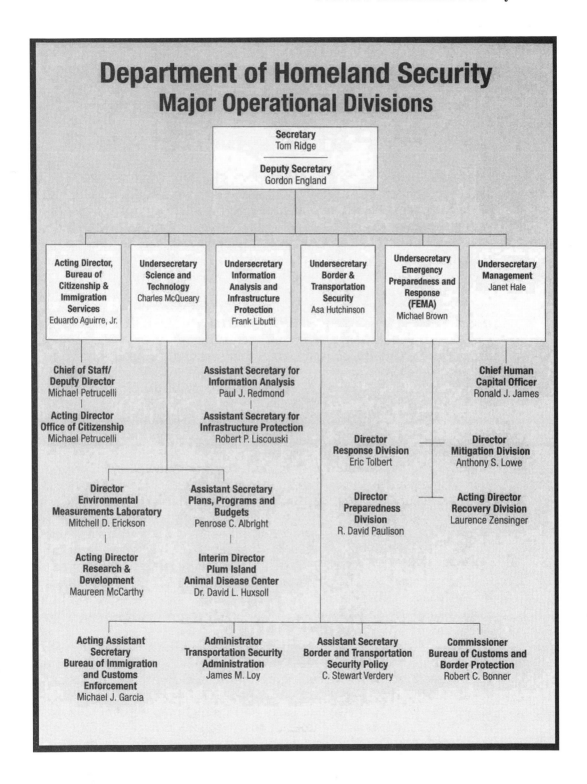

Department of Homeland Security
Major Operational Divisions

Secretary
Tom Ridge

Deputy Secretary
Gordon England

Acting Director, Bureau of Citizenship & Immigration Services
Eduardo Aguirre, Jr.

Undersecretary Science and Technology
Charles McQueary

Undersecretary Information Analysis and Infrastructure Protection
Frank Libutti

Undersecretary Border & Transportation Security
Asa Hutchinson

Undersecretary Emergency Preparedness and Response (FEMA)
Michael Brown

Undersecretary Management
Janet Hale

Chief of Staff/ Deputy Director
Michael Petrucelli

Assistant Secretary for Information Analysis
Paul J. Redmond

Chief Human Capital Officer
Ronald J. James

Acting Director Office of Citizenship
Michael Petrucelli

Assistant Secretary for Infrastructure Protection
Robert P. Liscouski

Director Response Division
Eric Tolbert

Director Mitigation Division
Anthony S. Lowe

Director Environmental Measurements Laboratory
Mitchell D. Erickson

Assistant Secretary Plans, Programs and Budgets
Penrose C. Albright

Director Preparedness Division
R. David Paulison

Acting Director Recovery Division
Laurence Zensinger

Acting Director Research & Development
Maureen McCarthy

Interim Director Plum Island Animal Disease Center
Dr. David L. Huxsoll

Acting Assistant Secretary Bureau of Immigration and Customs Enforcement
Michael J. Garcia

Administrator Transportation Security Administration
James M. Loy

Assistant Secretary Border and Transportation Security Policy
C. Stewart Verdery

Commissioner Bureau of Customs and Border Protection
Robert C. Bonner

Source: From "Is Homeland Security Keeping America Safe?" by Jeff Stein in *CQ Weekly* June 14, 2003. Copyright © 2003 Congressional Quarterly Inc.

Homeland Insecurity[3]

By Merrell Noden
Popular Science, September 2002

My first brush with terrorism came in 1973, when I was 18 and living in London on what the English call a working holiday. It was a weird time to be a teenager at large in the United Kingdom. London was under siege from a relentless IRA bombing campaign. Bobbies patrolled the streets for explosives. Posters and public announcements in the underground told Londoners to report suspicious bags. Bombs seemed to be going off everywhere, in cars and pubs and shopping arcades and telephone kiosks. Bomb threats were common—one was phoned into a Leicester Square movie theater while I was watching *The Sting*. On occasion I actually heard a distant explosion; more commonly, the wail of sirens. London was an exciting place to be; the bombs heightened the excitement, but did not seem directed at me, an invincible 18-year-old American.

On December 21, 1973, I went to a post office near Trafalgar Square to call my girlfriend back home. As I waited for a phone, I heard a loud thump, as if a huge fist had pounded on a drum the size of a house. A bomb, certainly, and to my ears it sounded like it might have been detonated right outside the post office, though in fact it had gone off more than a hundred yards away. I walked outside into noisy chaos familiar to anyone who has watched newscasts from Israel in recent months. Pulsing blue lights swept the darkness; police cars sped by in one direction and people fled in the other. This was too close, and I had no desire to linger. As I walked home up Charing Cross Road, wired with adrenaline, scanning parked cars with a horrible new interest, something had changed.

I had experienced the profound shift in understanding that can follow a brush with disaster: Where there had been a kind of blinkered, confident obliviousness, now there was a panicky conviction about my utter vulnerability.

On the morning of September 11, 2001, 19 hijackers boarded four jetliners, none having been stopped by the Swiss cheese operation that passed for airport security, and launched an attack that caused a nationwide shift in perception like the one I had experienced courtesy of the IRA. America suddenly had its technology turned against it with box cutters and domestic flight-school training. Pilots were murdered, transponders turned off, and commercial airplanes flown

---

into symbols of wealth, government, and military power—while high-tech U.S. defense systems desperately and fruitlessly tried to figure out what was going on.

Ever since, we've been told by our government to expect more attacks, with the addition of a handy color-coded system to tell us how nervous we should be. What we've not been told as often is that, at the big-city level, at ground zero, where so many Americans live, the degree of protection remains woefully low—not much better than it was before September 11. Much of the problem is money, and the will to find it. In a June survey, an overwhelming majority of city mayors claimed they lacked the resources and technology to protect their cities, with more than three-quarters saying they were unable to pay for detection and emergency-response equipment. That may begin to change this fall, thanks to a White House pledge of $3.5 billion to city, county, and state governments for first-responder technology and crews. That money would come a full year after the attacks.

What we have, in the starkest terms, is a national deficit in equipment, technology, and experience.

What we have, in the starkest terms, is a national deficit in equipment, technology, and experience. "None of us here ever anticipated such an attack as occurred on 9/11," admits Sgt. Steve Dixon of the San Jose police department. "So obviously we have never prepared for such a thing."

City police departments are struggling. "As far as technology is concerned," says R. Gil Kerlikowske, chief of the Seattle police department, "we simply don't have enough money to buy most of the advanced technology. We hope the federal government will help." Kerlikowske's first wish is not for portable radiation-detection equipment or gamma ray truck scanners like those being rushed into use in ports. He wants a better search engine for his computers, to ferret out license plate numbers from scattered arrest records.

This broad lack of preparedness at the urban level reflects that seen at U.S. airports on September 11. "The rest of the world," says Ian Gilchrist, former head of security at Hong Kong airport and now a consultant, "has had more than 20 years in which to evolve its security system following the era of hijackings in the late 1970s and the in-flight bombings of the early '80s. The United States was thinking, 'It will never happen here.' So, while the rest of the world was learning, thinking, growing, the United States did nothing."

What is difficult at airports is a thousand times harder, experts warned me, in cities. Airports are relatively small, controlled environments. Access can theoretically be limited until every passenger and employee passes through an eye-of-the-needle checkpoint. If security personnel are well-trained and equipped, it ought to be possible to keep an airport secure. Cities are big, open, sloppy systems, in which millions of people move about freely and unpredictably.

"We can't restrict the free movement and access of every single person that comes into this city," says Margret Kellems, who, as Washington, D.C.'s deputy mayor for public safety and justice, oversees the District's fire, police, and emergency response departments. "If somebody wants to strap dynamite to their chest and walk into a public space downtown, that's very difficult to detect. Obviously you try, you try to be aware."

Yet Washington has demonstrated that systematic technological responses to terrorist threats are possible at the urban level, money and will permitting. (Federal money helps.) Consider the D.C. transit system. Officials in Washington began evaluating its vulnerabilities in 1995, responding to the sarin nerve gas attack in the Tokyo subway, which killed 12 and injured thousands. Then in October 2001, D.C. officials asked Congress and the White House for $190 million for security enhancements. In April, they asked for an additional $107 million. Although so far they have received only $49 million, D.C. officials are putting their plans into action. They've purchased motion detectors for rail and bus yards in case someone tries to plant a time-delayed bomb; they've bought GPS-based Automatic Vehicle Locators that sound an alarm if a bus is driven off its planned route or is stolen from its yard at night. There is a pilot program to put digital cameras on buses, a plan to install fiber-optics to relay pictures from in-station closed-circuit (CCTV) cameras, and a drive to upgrade the public address systems in all Metro stations. This is a publicized initiative, and the public is being marshaled: D.C. Metro officials have distributed "Dear Fellow Rider" brochures, asking passengers to make suggestions on prepaid postcards.

The D.C. Metro is the first subway system in the world to be equipped with chemical weapons sensors.

The D.C. Metro is the first subway system in the world to be equipped with chemical weapons sensors. (Not even Tokyo has them.) Two stations had been fitted with them even before September 11; 10 more are now being outfitted and $20 million of that extra $107 million is earmarked for 15 further stations. Eventually, all stations may have the sensors, with biological-agent detectors retrofitted when available. In the event of a chemical attack, Metro is equipping not only its emergency response teams but all Metro workers with protective gear, including masks like those used in Israel. "Since the sarin gas attack of 1995 we have had a motto in our department never to toe-tag a first responder," says Metro Transit Police Chief Barry McDevitt.

Of course, Washington is a relatively small city, built to serve government. New York is massive and unruly. Early this year New York Mayor Michael Bloomberg appointed Frank Libutti, a former three-star Marine lieutenant general and special assistant for homeland security, to the new city post of deputy commissioner for counter-terrorism. The NYPD has hired an infectious disease specialist and created a board of doctors to advise on nuclear, chemical, and biological threats. What Libutti's group is up to is largely a secret. Although New Yorkers periodically hear bulletins about beefed up security—bridges and tunnels are occasionally shut down, or subject to stepped-up vehicle searches—and have witnessed massive police response to events like the World Economic Forum in late January and the July 4 fireworks, New York security officials are not keeping a high profile or handing out a lot of brochures. (Ads for a new antiterror hotline appeared in newspapers in June, but officials were not forthcoming.) Libutti was unavailable to talk to *Popular Science*, and, when asked if someone else could describe the antiterrorism strategy, a spokesman declined: "His office is made up of police officers, and police officers have never dealt with this issue before." Meanwhile, officials in Mayor Bloomberg's office refused to comment, though one conceded that there's not much to talk about until the cities, states, and the federal government agree to fund new technologies and address manpower needs. By summer, the hot topic was the new Department of Homeland Security.

The Port Authority, the agency that protects New York's bridges and tunnels, did say that things are being done: "We do have bomb-sniffing dogs, but I can't discuss what they are doing," said agency spokesperson Steve Coleman, adding that trucks and vans were being stopped and inspected, but only on a random basis now.

In late Spring I conducted a two-day walkabout in New York, eyeing infrastructure for signs of technological responses to 9/11. Accompanying me was Paul Quellin, an English consultant who managed security training at Manchester Airport for 10 years and was over here leading seminars for the U.S. Department of Energy. Granting that many changes to New York's security system may be invisible (beyond the deployment of soldiers in Penn Station and the like), what I saw with Quellin was . . . not much.

Consider the simple matter of garbage cans. In the D.C. Metro system, containers identified as potential receptacles for bombs were removed. In New York, Quellin immediately pointed to the black metal cans on the subway platforms as shrapnel waiting to happen. "The metal is the bomb," he told me, peering glumly into one. "Put enough explosive in these and you've got torn steel going 200 meters a second."

This is basic stuff: In England, where the IRA began using trash "bins" as bomb receptacles years ago, many outdoor bins now have a 2-inch lining of fiberglass-reinforced plastic, which contains the force of a blast and directs it skyward. Last year, an English company called Aigis Engineering Solutions began marketing indoor bins lined with a blast-absorption composite called TABRE topped by layers of water and air, a system that's designed to turn the blast into steam. D.C. officials earmarked a million dollars to buy explosive-resistant garbage cans from a company called Mistral Security, which has installed them in a number of New York public spaces, including Penn and Grand Central stations.

Or consider the more complex matter of protecting large urban office towers. Even in New York, building security, which tightened after 9/11, loosened not long after. "For a time after 9/11, we did spot-checks [of bags]," one manager of a business tower told me. He seemed resigned to a largely—though not necessarily unimportant—symbolic effort. "You have to be reasonable. The technology today means a bomb could be hidden in your cellphone or pager."

Adds a veteran Drug Enforcement Administration officer, now head of security at a midtown tower: "Everybody is looking for that silver bullet that will guarantee that if you do X, Y, or Z, you will be safe forever. It's not out there."

Much of the office tower security Quellin and I observed seemed haphazard at best, pointless at worst. At one landmark building I noticed that despite a sign proclaiming that all bags, briefcases, and

---

> *"Everybody is looking for that silver bullet that will guarantee that if you do X, Y, or Z, you will be safe forever. It's not out there."*—a
> **veteran DEA officer**

---

packages were subject to inspection, not a single one was actually inspected during the time I watched. Much of what passes for security in buildings consisted of looking at driver's licenses and employee ID cards.

"There's a mindset," says Ian Gilchrist, "within airports and in buildings too, favoring photo ID. It's being touted as a security measure. It has no security effect whatsoever." ID cards are easily forged or swapped, and, in the case of many building security checks, there is no link between ID cards and a database that might verify current employment. Driver's licenses and other state-issued IDs are dubious at best. More sophisticated biometric systems could be years away.

This matter of privacy in the prevention of terrorism illustrates a clear transatlantic divide. In Quellin's view, CCTV could improve security in a city like New York. While the structure and vast extent of the tunnels and platforms in the New York City subway system make the deployment of chemical weapon sensors along the D.C. model expensive and tricky, Manhattan's broad, straight avenues make it ideally suited to TV cameras—far more suited than London's cramped, winding streets. "You wouldn't need as many here," he said, "so it would be cheaper."

England is gaga over CCTV technology, although new debate has raged this summer about its efficacy; the *Guardian* reported that between 1996 and 1998 CCTV technology made up three-quarters of the Home Office crime prevention budget. The cameras were first deployed in number in the early '90s, at least partially in response to IRA bombings. When they seemed to have a deterrent effect on crime in general, and led to high-profile non-terrorist criminal convictions, the Brits installed more and more. There are some 150,000 cameras in London and the average Londoner supposedly appears on one or another of them 300 times a day. Surveillance, to Londoners, is a fact of life, and for many a comfort.

Less of a comfort to Americans. Here it is assumed that a citizen has the right to move through a public place without being watched—although surveillance is routine in many cities. In 1998 the New York Civil Liberties Union counted 2,397 surveillance cameras in Manhattan; a map is posted on the Web. The number has risen since then. Quellin spotted them everywhere, with more being installed: over doors, on roofs, overlooking fountains, at skating rinks and stadiums. Many cabs have them, as does my apartment building and even the nice little Greenwich Village restaurant where I eat lunch. (It's not only a New York thing: San Francisco's BART system is updating its 30-year-old CCTV technology, with color digital cameras already in use at one station and more due to come online in another by year's end.)

"It's interesting to hear Americans talk about their fear of CCTV," Quellin said with a smile, as we stood outside the New York Stock Exchange, gazing up at yet another of the smoked glass balls discreetly mounted on the corners of many New York buildings. "There's a lot of it here already."

The emphasis on CCTV highlights a key problem: manpower shortage. CCTVs provide a technological assist for what is essentially a beat-patrol job. "Most of what is available for outdoor security is meant to protect places where there isn't supposed to be normal vehicular or pedestrian traffic," says John Sczepanski, vice president for business development for Magal Security Systems, an Israeli firm. "There are electromagnetic sensors that can detect people or vehicles going over a surface, but those are meant for areas where there isn't supposed to be anybody. Fifth Avenue in New York? There's nothing you can do but put a lot of CCTV cameras in place and have someone monitoring it all the time."

Yes, radiation and bomb-detection equipment can be deployed on a limited basis for special events, or in stadium entrances, but these are impractical for routine public-space patrols. The director of emergency management in Indianapolis, for example, has outfitted robots with chemical detection equipment to augment handheld sensors at important events, but says, "We have no plans for permanent air-sampling equipment. We can't sample everything all the time." On New Year's Eve, the NYPD used handheld radiation monitors borrowed from the U.S. Customs Service to screen the crowd in Times Square. But day-to-day security is accomplished by a crew of 52 security officers who walk the streets, serving as the eyes and ears of the police.

Today, most CCTV cameras simply record. No one is watching; tape is studied after the fact. But Americans don't want to see tape of the next Mohamed Atta breezing toward his date with destiny. Spotting suspects or suspicious behavior in real time is the challenge. Personnel hired to watch cameras bore easily; software is needed to recognize individuals or trouble, and alert staff. Into this category falls facial recognition software such as that developed by Identix, a Minnesota biometric technology company, which got a lot of attention on Memorial Day weekend when its software was used to scan crowds visiting the Statue of Liberty.

> *Low-tech solutions can be among the most effective for deterrence, detection, and response.*

The ACLU blasted the Identix test, calling it an insult to the nation's beacon of liberty, and warned that the software fails to identify people who are threats while turning up many false positives. In Washington, at a June City Council meeting to discuss creating an integrated network of CCTVs by linking police, subway, and school cameras, an ACLU lawyer warned that "there is no record of the [150,000 cameras in London] being involved in the apprehension of a single terrorist." (Later he conceded there may be one case, a 1993 bombing at Harrods caught on film, which led to arrests.)

Manufacturers and supporters wave away the privacy concerns: "There's a way this can be done where it doesn't violate civil liberties," insists Identix spokesman Meir Kahtan. "The camera isn't looking for you or me. It's looking for that small group on the Watch List. If there's no match, it doesn't keep your face."

Another strategy uses CCTV technology to spot trouble in real time. The Cromatica program from the Digital Imaging Research Centre at London's Kingston University looks for anomalies in pedestrian traffic flow: people stopping for long periods, people running, or crowds bunching. It alerts staff, who zero in and decide whether the situation warrants police attention. It also spots unattended baggage and, using its memory function, finds the person who left it. The program has been used, with promising early results, the designers say, in London's Liverpool Street train station.

The new element in all this is terror by suicide. In Israel, suicide attacks have been devastatingly effective against police efforts. Nor are bombproof bins a help if the terrorist is the bomb (though there is nothing to indicate that would be the approach on U.S. soil). Whether against a single McVeigh-style extremist or a group with grandiose ambitions, there is no magical-technological solution to the threat to cities. There is no prophylactic bubble of integrated warning systems that would shield a city—a localized Star Wars, if you will—providing early warnings of all biological, chemical, or explosive threats as they approach.

"If that were possible," notes Robert Strang, a former DEA agent working for Decision Strategies, a global security and investigation firm, "Israel would have it. The real goal, the real answer, is intelligence. We've got to be aggressive about knowing what's going on in these terrorist criminal organizations."

Hence the focus on the failures of intelligence gathering in the period before September 11. However secure harbors and airports and other points of urban entry can be made—and for the foreseeable future there will be many holes—improved intelligence is vital.

Most experts I talked to were as concerned about training and legwork as technology. They noted that low-tech solutions can be among the most effective for deterrence, detection, and response: bomb-sniffing dogs (eight more in training for the D.C. Metro system, bringing its total to 11); better communication systems (two-way wireless radios with e-mail pagers for command staff in Indianapolis); more information and heightened awareness (information about weaponized diseases circulated to physicians in San Jose); and evacuation drills. These may not be as sexy as facial recognition software and air-sniffing robots, but, as Strang points out, "Tens of thousands of lives were spared on 9/11 because people didn't just sit at their desks when the alarm went off." Dozens of others, mostly firemen, died because police and fire radio systems did not work together.

Unlike my friends in London, and the Israelis who send newborns home with gas masks, we're new to all this. "It's going to be a major change for Americans over the next 10 years," says Strang. "Obviously, this problem is here to stay and we are unfortunately now part of this global problem."

But September 11 also left room to reflect on the strength of cities. The size, disorder, and vitality of our cities make them hard to protect, but also extraordinarily resilient. As horrible as the attacks were, they neither stopped nor much slowed down Washington and New York. Security systems utterly let us down, but the response to the emergency was heroic. The remarkable thing is not that the attacks on these cities happened; it's that, in a crucial way, they failed.

Detecting the Threat

Technology and the War on Terror[4]

By Shane Harris
Government Executive, July 2002

When Jim Furnish stands next to the radioactive cesium, his hip starts to tickle. On his belt, where most people clip wireless pagers or cellular phones, Furnish wears a black detector roughly the size of a calculator that vibrates whenever he gets close to radioactive material. Furnish is a Customs Service inspector at the Ports of Los Angeles and Long Beach, Calif., and he says the most surprising things can set the detector off.

Smoke alarms, for example, contain radioactive chemicals that make the detector very excited, he tells me. And then, of course, there's the scanner that Furnish and his colleagues use to inspect 20-foot-long shipping containers. It uses cesium to produce a powerful gamma ray that enables inspectors to see through the thick steel walls of the containers, the way doctors use X-rays to see bones through skin. So Furnish stays clear of the scanner when possible, but hovers next to the containers, serving as a human Geiger counter. The thing that he least wants to find in those containers would set his detector to buzzing wildly: a nuclear bomb.

It's fitting that Furnish works about 30 miles from Hollywood, because his job is straight out of an action film. He'd probably blush if compared to a screen icon, but he would agree that his life has become a real drama since Sept. 11. For almost a year now, Furnish and his fellow inspectors have been scanning and prodding about 100 shipping containers a day with gamma rays, fiber-optic cameras and chemical swipe kits, because Customs officials fear that terrorists will try to use one of the 5 million containers that arrive in U.S. ports every year as a carrier pigeon for a weapon of mass destruction.

No one wants that to happen less than Furnish. On the morning I visited him at the L.A. side of the port, he showed me Customs' main defensive weapon, a white pickup truck rigged with a 15-foot steel boom that juts out from the cab, parallel to the ground like a stiff arm. At the end of the boom hangs a white metal box that houses the cesium that sets off Furnish's detector if he gets too close.

---

4. Article by Shane Harris from *Government Executive* July 2002. Copyright © National Journal Group, Inc. Reprinted with permission.

Inspectors position a container under the boom, place the radio-active source box on one side, and slowly drive forward, taking a picture of the container's innards as they go. Inside the truck, another inspector, Jerry Gomez, sits in an extra-wide back seat in front of a desktop computer. If a bomb is hidden in a container, it's Gomez's job to find it.

> *Technology is the backbone of the nation's homeland security.*

The containers Gomez scans have been singled out for inspection by Customs agents using a software program that correlates the container's port of origin, the recipient of its cargo and whether the shipping company is a first-time importer to the United States. About 2 percent of all containers are pulled aside each year after being processed through this threat matrix.

A flatbed truck pulls a container between Gomez's truck and his gamma beam. Gomez pulls out his radio and gives an order to another inspector on the dock: "Light the candle." He turns to me and says, "We're about to get hot." Instantly and silently, the gamma ray beam pierces the container. The truck inches forward, scanning the length of the container, and eight seconds later, an image has been painted across Gomez's monitor. An outline of vague shapes, alternating between dark and light, the image is indistinguishable until Gomez adjusts the contrast. Suddenly, the true picture is revealed: Tires. Piles and piles of rubber tires.

If there were anything in that container that didn't look round or tire-like, Gomez would order a closer look. Instead, he clears the container to its destination. Customs inspectors have found drugs, money and stowaways inside these boxes over the years, but they've yet to find a weapon, nuclear or otherwise, or the materials to make one. But Gomez believes the day is coming. "I'm confident that we will find something," he says. "I know it."

Customs inspectors like Furnish and Gomez are links in a long, overlapping chain of law enforcement officers, disease specialists, criminal investigators and intelligence analysts, who for years before Sept. 11 counted terrorist attacks among their list of worries, but never placed them at the top. Now, their lives have changed, as has their mission.

While the Bush administration struggles to come up with a precise definition of homeland security, and a plan for how to achieve it, an army of front-line personnel has set up trenches in airports, shipyards, border crossings and hospitals. They've armed themselves with a vast arsenal of technological weapons. Customs inspectors' gamma beams and radiation alarms, which 4,000 of them wear today, are but some of those armaments, which range from the bleeding edge of innovation to the decidedly low-tech.

But while the war on terror continues to evolve and the enemy remains elusive, one thing is certain: Technology is the backbone of the nation's homeland security, and the soldiers who use it are girding for a fight.

Most of the technologies agencies employ to secure the homeland have been used for a long time, so the people who work with them know their strengths and weaknesses. Customs inspectors, for example, search for bombs with handheld sensors first used in the 1980s during the drug war to find concealed packages of narcotics. The scanners detect sudden changes in density, a tip-off that a brick of explosives might be hidden behind a container wall, but they're not useful for finding objects buried deep within other materials.

While sophisticated technologies are worthless in the hands of clumsy users, everyday toolbox items can become finely tuned detective instruments in the hands of a brilliant inspector. One such person is Ray Pardo, a senior Customs inspector. Far outside his home base in Newark, N.J., the busiest seaport on the East Coast, Pardo has developed an iconic reputation for foiling smugglers who take enormous pains to hide contraband material. It seems there's almost no smuggling trick that Pardo can't beat. So of course, Customs officials want him on the front lines of the new war.

Pardo has created a cadre of home-grown technologies to find hidden items on his own, while private corporations with teams of engineers have failed to bring their own anti-smuggling gadgets to market.

Consider one technology firm that has tried unsuccessfully for years to market to the government an acoustic identification device, a machine that uses sound waves to locate concealed objects. The objects resonate when struck with the waves, creating unique audio signatures. Bricks of cocaine might sound might one way, bricks of explosives another.

But while the company has spent untold sums on research, development and marketing, Pardo has already developed a similar tool in his workshop using a compressed-air hammer and a stethoscope. Banging about with his contraption, he has uncovered cocaine stashes buried deep inside giant rolls of paper. With a quick adjustment of the device, Pardo says he could find metal bomb components the same way.

Pardo's toolshed ingenuity has earned him the nickname "MacGyver" among his colleagues after the fictitious television adventurer famous for fashioning radios from paper clips and making boomerangs out of bubble gum. Others have affectionately nicknamed Pardo "Inspector Gadget." But for all his natural talent and the devoted following he's attracted, Pardo recoils when labeled a genius, even when standing in the makeshift museum inspectors have set up as a tribute to some of his biggest busts.

Perhaps Pardo sloughs off the accolades because he knows other people face more daunting challenges. Pardo can spend days devising a strategy to outwit a terrorist, but other agents and inspectors don't have the luxury of time. They're staring down potential terrorists every moment, quite literally looking them in the face.

At the Los Angeles International Airport, INS inspectors look at more than 25,000 sets of eyes a day. Each pair could belong to a business traveler, a new immigrant or a terrorist. Inspectors have precious few technologies to help them tell the difference.

Five thousand immigrants arrive at the airport each month, more than at any other airport in the country. Each year, 8.5 million people move through one of about 70 immigration booths staffed by inspectors who spend less than a minute with each of them. Before Sept. 11, the INS was actually required to process a plane load of passengers in less than 45 minutes.

There is one kind of technology that, more than any other, could significantly improve the INS' ability to keep potential terrorists out of the country, L.A. Port Director Thomas Graber tells me: biometrics.

Biometrics is the identification of a person by his or her unique characteristics, such as a fingerprint or the shape of the retina. At the INS, the use of biometric technology is in its infancy. The agency has tried to initiate a biometrics regime at the Mexican border, but officials have yet to install machines to read fingerprints on cards issued to thousands of Mexican citizens. An agency spokeswoman says the INS will soon deploy machines at some ports of entry along the United States' southern border.

Inspectors at the L.A. airport scan most passports through an electronic reader that decodes passenger information embedded in the document. They match the name on the passport against a passenger manifest from the airline, and they also compare the name for matches in INS databases of wanted immigration offenders. The holes in that system are huge.

For one thing, Graber says, passports can be falsified. Only biometrics can truly identify someone. For example, if passports required fingerprints, it would be simple to determine whether a fingerprint belonged to the person holding the passport. Also, not all names on various terrorist watch lists kept by some agencies are fed into the INS system. In June, news reports revealed that two of the suspected Sept. 11 hijackers, who the CIA knew were terrorists, weren't put on any watch list until a few weeks before the attack.

As Graber walks down the long line of inspection booths, he is greeted with smiles and handshakes from people he sees every day. He's candid about his agency's shortcomings, but he's also a firm believer in the power of his people to overcome their situation, as they have before.

Three years ago, inspectors were so bogged down filling out and filing immigration forms by hand that one enterprising employee built a software program in his spare time to catalog such records automatically. INS officials applauded his creation, called Case Track, and gave Graber permission to export the system to 12 other airports under a pilot program.

If Graber could have his wish, every inspector would be able to scan a passport, immediately pull up several biometric identifiers and send a digital fingerprint taken at the booth to the FBI's criminal database to look for an instant match. The INS and the FBI are inching toward that day, having begun last year to link up their respective fingerprint databanks of immigration violators and convicted criminals. But that project was supposed to have begun two years ago.

Until the technology revolution begins at INS, Graber patiently waits, but some of his colleagues are anxious. As one inspector tells me, they want all the help they can get: "We need the supercomputers here."

Syndromic surveillance ... [is] a specialized offshoot of public health science that is being tapped in efforts to counter biological warfare.

Security experts warn that even the best technology never replaces basic common sense. They say a healthy dose of suspicion—someone's gut hunch to look closer at a situation—is more valuable than the most elegant technology scheme.

Still, a number of federal officials involved in homeland security efforts say they want tools that can take seemingly meaningless information and place it in the context of a larger picture; the hope is that computers could help predict attacks before they occur. The government is years away from implementing such sophisticated systems on a wide scale. But if agency leaders want to see where some of these tools are just starting to be tested, they might look to the investigators who are on the lookout for the most frightening kind of attack of all.

On the second floor of the Los Angeles County Department of Health Services, which sits on a drab and lifeless stretch of Figueroa Street in the downtown business district, a team of epidemiologists combs through emergency room reports, lab results and physicians' diagnoses looking for the possibility that terrorists have unleashed an outbreak of smallpox, anthrax, salmonella or some other deadly pathogen. The signals they watch for aren't always obvious. Disease experts note that the reactions to a bioterrorist attack would probably first appear as flu-like symptoms in a small group of people. A single patient complaining to his doctor of sudden diarrhea and headaches means nothing. Doctors treat such cases all the time. But 10 cases, all in the same emergency room, could indicate an outbreak has begun.

The art of monitoring reports of symptoms over a vast geographic area is known as syndromic surveillance. It's a specialized offshoot of public health science that is being tapped in efforts to counter biological warfare. For the past three years, scientists in Los Angeles and other cities, as well as at the Centers for Disease Control and Prevention in Atlanta, have steadily increased their use of technology to create a vast surveillance network, an eye in the sky that could alert individual physicians to a larger threat brewing around them.

The Los Angeles County bioterrorism team, with some grants from the CDC, has developed a series of online symptom collection systems that they're now integrating into what will eventually become a Web-based communications device for doctors, health care workers and emergency responders during an attack.

They call it the Health Alert System Training and Education Network, or HASTEN. On the day I visited with the chief of the team, Dr. Laurene Mascola, a half dozen employees were using the system's precursor—which collects patient diagnoses from hospitals and doctors' offices—to track an outbreak of salmonella linked to tainted Mexican cantaloupe. Such small outbreaks are easy to monitor and contain, Mascola says. But she knows fighting a bioterror attack would be a nightmare.

Public hysteria is one of the biggest problems epidemiologists would have to contend with. Los Angeles epidemiologists got a glimpse of it during last October's anthrax attacks, which occurred on the other side of the country. Mascola recalls trying to fill a tetracycline prescription for a family member and being told by her pharmacist that all supplies of the drug had been snatched up by Los Angelenos terrified they'd been exposed to anthrax spores in the mail. And federal health officials, fearing a run on the anthrax-busting antibiotic Cipro, threatened to revoke the manufacturer's patent and let the government manufacture the drug.

The HASTEN system would help stem pandemonium at least by keeping public health officials apprised of an outbreak's progress, so that they, too, don't give in to panic. Doctors and other health workers would report symptoms into the main database. Then, when signals of an outbreak were spotted, alerts would automatically be e-mailed to epidemiologists or sent by wireless phones and handheld computers. County health officials already get such messages from other online systems.

The CDC uses a system like HASTEN that was developed by a team of technology firms in Northern Virginia. Known as the Lightweight Epidemiological Advanced Detection and Emergency Response System (LEADERS), the Web-based surveillance program was used by CDC disease experts in Manhattan emergency rooms immediately after the Sept. 11 attacks. It was also deployed in Arizona at the last World Series and in Los Angeles during the 2000 Democratic National Convention.

There are two big shortcomings in any syndromic surveillance system, according to a former CDC bioterrorism expert who asked to remain anonymous. First, diseases are discovered only after they've occurred. Surveillance isn't about prevention as much as containment. Second, hospitals report symptoms using different terminology. CDC epidemiologists in New York on Sept. 11 entered data into LEADERS on their own using a set of common terms, the expert says. That avoided confusion, but it also kept the epidemiologists from doing their investigative work. They were too busy entering data to talk to many patients.

Rather than relying on the CDC to operate the surveillance system, the expert suggests that local teams be trained to use the technology and spot problems at the local level, as health officials are doing in Los Angeles. Failing that, the system needs to be simple to use.

When the CDC installed LEADERS in Los Angeles during the Democratic convention, emergency room physicians used touch-screen monitors and answered simple questions with yes and no answers, says Dr. Eric Noji, the associate director of CDC's Bioterrorism Preparedness and Response Program and one of the world's foremost experts in "disaster medicine." Noji says health officials have advanced in the bioterror war by developing rapid testing kits that can confirm a disease in a matter of days, instead of weeks. But "other than awareness and maybe a little more application of technology, we're not a tremendous amount ahead of where we were on September 11," he says.

Noji says a top priority now is to create a national biodefense system, a network of sensors placed in highly trafficked public areas, such as subways, that would "detect a chemical weapon or a biological weapon before anybody has gotten it on their skin or body." There is technology to do that, he says, but it has to be enhanced. "[It's] at the Wright Brothers level compared with a B-1 stealth bomber," he says. The proposed Homeland Security Department would lead the effort to develop such a system. Noji says it will take about 10 years.

A layered regime, perhaps of syndromic surveillance, a sensor network and testing to quickly determine what's making people sick, could serve as a model for an effective strategy to fight bioterrorism, with advanced technology as its underpinning. But, Noji cautions, no system functions without perceptive and capable people to run it. "More important than any technology—even if you've got supercomputers—the most important link in the chain is the alert clinician."

Earlier this year, as agencies awaited the release of the Office of Homeland Security's national strategy, technology's role in the plan was already taking shape. But many agencies have some big technological hurdles ahead. Investments in technology haven't been a high priority at every agency. The Customs Service spent heavily over the past three years to acquire new tools for the drug war. But the CDC allocated only $50 million in 1999 to help state and local governments with their anti-bioterrorism programs; technological upgrades accounted for only one portion of that figure. And as recent events have shown, the FBI's investment in anti-terror technologies has been as paltry as its funding of basic information systems throughout the bureau.

Compounding the problem, the government's share of funding for the research and development of new products has been eclipsed by venture capital funding in the private sector. And many niche technology firms, whose products might help secure the homeland, refuse to sign government contracts because the agreements often restrict their ability to sell to the commercial market.

Technology itself can't prevent terrorism. People are the key ingredient. Without human intelligence and communication on the front end, technology is worthless. Artificial intelligence still is the stuff of science fiction. Groundbreaking work on neural networks

---

> *Without human intelligence and communication on the front end, technology is worthless.*

---

has so far been carried out only in limited, discrete ways, such as looking for patterns of credit card transactions to detect potential fraud. The technology isn't ready for homeland security duty, many experts believe.

The lasting effect of new homeland security technologies will likely be to improve government's ability to function well in areas that have nothing to do with preventing terrorism. Stronger health surveillance, for example, will help doctors better control naturally occurring outbreaks of disease, an effect that some local health officials are already seeing as they employ new monitoring systems. Biometric devices at border crossings will speed the flow of immigrant traffic more often than they will catch terrorists trying to enter the country. But when it comes to thwarting terrorists, one industry executive says, the best technology can do is "even the odds."

It's hard to find anyone, especially on the front lines, who thinks that would be a bad thing.

The General Nobody Knows[5]

By Michael Hirsh
Newsweek, July 14, 2003

It's a blistering day on the plains of Colorado, and Gen. Ed Eberhart strides into his brand-new "situational awareness center" at Northern Command. Eberhart may be the most powerful man in America nobody has really heard of: he's in charge of military deployments against domestic terror. A frisson of activity fills the room. In seconds every soldier is either standing or halfway out of his computer console. Eberhart's staff doesn't get to see him much: in the nine months since NORTHCOM was created, he's been to dozens of states, visiting National Guard and Coast Guard bases, local fire, police and paramedic units, even Rotary Clubs—forging the loose network that might respond to a domestic terror attack. Eberhart waves his team back to their places. The duty officer is at his side. "Everything quiet?" Eberhart asks amiably, eying the array of flat computer screens on the front wall. "Anything new down in Arizona?" "Nothing new on the fires right now, sir. We're monitoring a suspicious package found on a New York subway." Eberhart nods, his ruddy face inscrutable. He gives no orders. There isn't anything he can do.

Soon Eberhart will be back to meeting and greeting locals again. Next month he redeploys to Las Vegas, where he'll join with civilian officials in a giant exercise involving a hypothetical terror strike (even President George W. Bush will have a part). For an ex-fighter pilot who also commands NORAD, the ultrasecret cold-war defense complex buried in nearby Cheyenne Mountain, starting up NORTHCOM has been as much about politics as spit and polish. In one sense, it's the kind of thing U.S. commanders haven't had to address since Union generals puzzled over what to do about the rebellious ladies of the Confederacy. How should American soldiers behave when deployed among Americans? Eberhart's forces won't be occupying U.S. cities—his mantra is that NORTHCOM doesn't move until asked by local, state or federal civilian authorities—but he knows NORTHCOM has "a different mission set" than the other four U.S. regional commands around the globe.

Mainly, Eberhart is keen to show he's sensitive to the deepest of American fears, that the military might wrest control from civilians. The Posse Comitatus Act of 1878 bars U.S. troops from enforcing U.S. laws. "It's the elephant in the room," says Rep. Jane Harman, the ranking Democrat on the Select Intelligence Committee, who

---

joined a congressional trip to Eberhart's headquarters in Colorado Springs last month to figure out just what NORTHCOM is up to. ("Nobody really knows it exists yet," says Rep. Jennifer Dunn.) But, Harman adds, the Posse Comitatus ban "is not absolute. It's like the First Amendment. You can't cry fire in a crowded theater and you can't always block the U.S. military on U.S. soil."

Eberhart seems the perfect message man to allay such anxieties. Lean in his flight suit, with a rugged face and thatch of white hair that evoke everyone's idea of a Hollywood general, the low-talking Eberhart could probably give his boss, Donald Rumsfeld, a few lessons in diplomacy, judging from the reaction of those who meet him. The general, who flew 300 combat missions in Vietnam, "is a remarkable man, a great leader," gushes Dunn. Even the no-nonsense Harman dubs him "charismatic."

NORTHCOM, which oversees North America, Mexico and parts of the Caribbean, was rushed into existence with little ado last year. Instituted on Oct. 1, 2002, it reaches "full operating capability" this October. That mainly means a headquarters staff of 500 and the NORAD air-defense system, but Eberhart notes that, like CENTCOM in Iraq under Gen. Tommy Franks, he has an array of forces at his disposal should Rumsfeld decide he needs them. Eberhart won't say how many troops he now commands, but "we're not talking about mass here."

Eberhart has clear authority to police the skies for terror and to scramble jets in response.

He admits that what he's doing at NORTHCOM couldn't be further from the traditional NORAD role: watching out for Soviet bogies from a superhardened base, away from the public eye. Not surprisingly—since the war that generals know best is always the last one—Eberhart sounds most confident in addressing a 9/11–style hijacking. Eberhart has clear authority to police the skies for terror and to scramble jets in response. If an airliner is hijacked and becomes a guided missile as on 9/11, only one option remains: to shoot it down. But he runs through all the precautions NORTHCOM would take to avert that: waiting to see if the passengers can wrest control, or the hijackers change their minds. About half of the training exercises he runs, he says, involve a language misunderstanding. Without saying so outright, he indicates that he could order a shoot-down himself.

Some congressional skeptics like Democratic Rep. Loretta Sanchez say there need to be more hearings and oversight on NORTHCOM's role. "There was never any debate about it," she says. But most praise Eberhart's efforts. "They're way ahead of Homeland Security in analyzing intelligence," says Sanchez. Indeed, Eberhart is intent on redressing the biggest breakdown of 9/11, the failure to pass on intel. Last week Baltimore Police Commissioner Kevin Clark, as part of a critique of Homeland Security efforts, angrily noted he often still hears about the latest threats on CNN. "Let's get past all the [security] clearances," he said.

Eberhart says he's doing that. "We first try to make sure all this is being shared," he says. "Our first question to the FBI is 'Does whoever needs to know, know that?' You name the state." Before long, Ed Eberhart will have been to them all.

II. Local Security and First Responders

Editors' Introduction

"**F**irst responders"—a term still awaiting inclusion in the dictionary—are the local police officers, firefighters, EMS workers, and hospital personnel who would be initially involved in the event of a terrorist attack, racing to the scene, rescuing survivors, controlling fires and toxic emissions, treating the wounded, and evacuating nearby areas. The public thinks of "first responders" as heroes, and they are, but they are also tired and worried as they try to prepare for an almost unimaginable range of emergencies with limited funds, equipment, and man-hours at their disposal.

"'First Responders' Find Their Jobs Even Tougher," from the *Dallas Morning News*, provides a good overview of the challenges facing local emergency teams today. They must develop new skills, learn to evaluate ominous, vaguely worded warnings, and stretch dollars and staff to the limit. And they must go forward, whether additional funds arrive on schedule or not. In "Their 9/11 Response: Be Prepared," from the *Los Angeles Times*, Richard T. Cooper concentrates on three individuals—a police commander, a doctor, and a fire chief—who were involved in the emergency response to 9/11. All three men have carried over memories and lessons from that day into their present positions, and all have worked at the grass-roots level for better preparedness. In "Are State and Local 'First Responders' Getting the Federal Funding They Say They Need?" from *CQ Weekly*, David Clarke examines the intricacies of government funding: the political and jurisdictional rivalries that can slow the release of money, the sleight of hand that can finance one program by cutting another, and the formulas for payout, so frequently disputed. (A chart of monies given for police and fire to the different states as of April 2003 is also included. How much of that money actually reaches local precincts, in the form of salaries or equipment, is another matter.) Disputes also arise between state and local governments concerning the distribution of funds, as states argue that the localities, without a comprehensive plan, would probably waste money on equipment and programs that were incompatible with those of neighboring localities. Since compatibility—networked technology—is a key issue, the federal government is currently siding with the states, although it has moved to limit the amounts they can retain.

Compatibility is the subject of Ellen Perlman's "Can We Talk?" from *Governing*, a journal for administrators. No one can forget how firefighters died at the World Trade Center because they could not receive, on their radios, the evacuation orders the police were broadcasting just before the Twin Towers collapsed. Getting all the emergency services on the same wavelength has become an overriding priority. Perlman examines the problem in detail (every step is beset with practical questions) and describes what some states and localities have accomplished. She also addresses wider issues of communication, as between different agencies and authorities.

Finally, in "Pounds of Cure," from *American City & County*, Kim O'Connell discusses preparedness in America's hospitals. Although most people do not think of hospital personnel as "first responders," doctors and nurses are immediately involved whenever disaster strikes. Moreover, if deadly germs were deliberately released into the general population, hospitals and public health agencies would be the first to know and the primary—perhaps the only—sources of treatment and protection. O'Connell describes the surveillance and monitoring programs that some localities have adopted for identifying suspect outbreaks of disease, and the plans for regional response—mass vaccinations, for example—that others are developing. Again, vigilance, information-sharing, and forethought seem to be the essential elements of security.

"First responders," of course, have plenty to do besides prepare for another 9/11. Thousands of smaller emergencies require, and receive, their attention every day. The extra efforts that local crews are making now to improve their communications, broaden their training, and extend the boundaries of preparedness for the sake of homeland security will also make a difference at the day-to-day emergency response level, where most of their work is still done.

"First Responders" Find Their Jobs Even Tougher[1]

BY ED TIMMS
THE DALLAS MORNING NEWS, SEPTEMBER 12, 2003

Across the nation, police officers, firefighters and other emergency personnel are on the front lines of a war against terrorism. Their jobs—already difficult—instantly became more complicated and demanding after the Sept. 11 attacks.

The enemy is largely unseen. The list of potential targets is staggering. Information about specific threats sometimes trickles down to the state and local level, if it makes it there at all.

Many of the nation's "first responders" have worked long hours of overtime because of terrorism alerts issued by the federal government and local reports of possible attacks, and as local communities scrambled to reduce their vulnerability. Because of concerns that chemical or biological weapons might be unleashed within the United States, they've had to learn new skills.

And for the communities they serve, paying for homeland security hasn't been easy, especially when many state and local governments are grappling with declining revenues and slashing their budgets.

"The mission of law enforcement has changed dramatically and we've had to undergo training that's very different from anything we've had before," said Farmers Branch Police Chief Jimmy Fawcett, president of the Texas Police Chiefs Association. "We're having to try to find funds for the equipment that we need. . . . And that is coming on top of budget constraints because of a very poor economy."

Federal Reaction

The nation's response after 9/11 may be best described as a work in progress. Local and federal authorities are still developing their strategies.

Perhaps the most significant response to the terrorist attacks and continuing threats was the creation of the Department of Homeland Security. The department was to take a more focused and streamlined approach to homeland defense, combining the skills and responsibilities of nearly two dozen federal agencies. It analyzes threats and intelligence and serves as a conduit of infor-

---

1. Article by Ed Timms from *The Dallas Morning News* September 12, 2003. Copyright © *The Dallas Morning News*. Reprinted with permission.

mation to state and local authorities. The department posts color-coded alerts to help the public gauge the terrorist threat level in the United States.

The State Department warned Wednesday of possible Al Qaeda attacks against U.S. interests, but the nation's terrorism alert level was not raised.

As it took on the daunting task of shoring up the nation's defenses, the department was criticized for perceived missteps and shortcomings.

"It has never been clearer that the role of our country's state and municipal emergency responders is as demanding and dangerous as ever," Sen. Patrick Leahy of Vermont, the ranking Democrat on the Senate Judiciary Committee, said at a recent hearing. "It is also clearer than ever that these real-life heroes out on the front lines every day are lacking the federal support they need and deserve to protect us."

In recent public appearances, Homeland Security Secretary Tom Ridge has pointed to several new initiatives aimed at improving security while acknowledging that that the work is far from complete.

"Every day, Homeland Security works to deliver on our mission to better prevent, prepare and respond to a terrorist attack," he said at the American Enterprise Institute this month.

The relative success or shortcomings of a specific federal or local agency often are in the eye of the beholder. Few who play an active role in homeland defense would deny that more needs to be done, and in some cases, perhaps not as much.

> *Few who play an active role in homeland defense would deny that more needs to be done, and in some cases, perhaps not as much.*

The Strain of Alerts

Especially in the months that followed 9/11, many first responders were overwhelmed with reports of possible terrorist plots and acts. Soon afterward, a relatively small number of anthrax-contaminated letters set off a panic that further stressed the nation's emergency response system.

And as new information about possible attacks was uncovered, the federal government issued terrorism alerts that also resulted in more work, and more angst, for police, firefighters and other emergency personnel.

Some state and local agencies, faced with mounting overtime bills and exhausted staffs, have tempered their response to the terrorist alerts.

"We take a very close look at the information we receive and correlate it to the intelligence information we have that's state-specific," said Frank Navarrete, Arizona's homeland security director. "And then we make a prudent decision as to whether to follow suit, or not follow suit."

Similarly, Bill Gross, Dallas' emergency preparedness coordinator, said that the city takes a more measured response to terrorist alerts, assessing whether the threat is "Dallas-specific."

Texas Homeland Security coordinator Jay Kimbrough said the deployment of forces is now more "credibility-based."

"Early on, it was almost a panic-based deployment," he said.

The manner in which information about potential threats is disseminated, however, is a point of contention between federal officials and local authorities.

"I think that the feds are doing better and they're working very hard to try to create more open channels of communication between federal intelligence agencies. But there's still very little structure in place to communicate up and down," said former Virginia Gov. Jim Gilmore, who heads the Congressional Advisory Panel to Assess Domestic Response Capabilities for Terrorism Involving Weapons of Mass Destruction, more simply known as the Gilmore Commission.

A Lack of Specifics

What terrorists will use, and when, and where, are critical questions. But intelligence gathering is an inexact science, and even if lines of communication are seamless, it's likely that some alerts warning of possible terrorist threats will be based on information that is not specific.

Communities continue to improve their coordination efforts, recognizing that a terrorist attack may not be confined to one city or county.

"What are they to do, not broadcast the threat at all?" Mr. Kimbrough said. "They're sort of caught in a difficult situation, whether to withhold the information because it doesn't cover a specific geographic area, or put the information out. I, for one, would prefer that they go ahead and put the information out."

Communities continue to improve their coordination efforts, recognizing that a terrorist attack may not be confined to one city or county. Mr. Gross said Texas communities increasingly are approaching homeland defense issues from a regional perspective.

In the past, he said, police and fire departments entered into mutual aid agreements, but with significant constraints.

"It was pretty much, 'If I'm not doing anything and I don't see a threat, and you're in trouble, I'll go help you. But if you're in trouble and I see something that's going to hurt me, I'm going to stay home and take care of me,'" Mr. Gross said. "That's been the standard mutual aid concept for some time."

Communication Trouble

Simply talking to one another is an issue in many communities. Police officers in adjoining cities, for example, may be unable to directly communicate with each other by radio during a terrorist attack because of incompatible systems. Different emergency response agencies within the same city may not be able to radio each other directly; that was the case in New York on Sept. 11, 2001.

"I can talk to Carrollton. I can talk to Addison. I can talk to Lewisville," Chief Fawcett said. "I have no ability to directly talk with the largest agency in the area, and that's Dallas."

Radio traffic between communities with incompatible communications systems can be channeled through dispatch centers, he said, but that's a cumbersome and time-consuming process.

Short of Help

Staffing is another issue in many communities where, in spite of the increased demands created by the threat of terrorism, the number of emergency personnel has actually decreased since 9/11. Local communities, as well as the federal government, are constrained by their budgets.

Harold Schaitberger, president of the International Association of Fire Fighters, recently noted that New York City has 500 fewer firefighters. Two-thirds of the nation's fire departments, he said, are understaffed and do not meet national standards.

Chief Fawcett said that after 9/11, "we started hearing about all this money that was going to start flowing."

"All that money didn't flow," he said. "I think the public believes that we got it, but it just didn't happen." Limited funding is now "trickling down," he said, but communities still have tremendous needs.

"How are we going to keep our people prepared and have the equipment?" he said. "It doesn't do any good to train them if you don't have the equipment to deal with the possible attacks that you're facing."

Texas has received $310 million in federal grants over the last two years to deal with terrorist attacks. However, one assessment concluded that Texas communities needed nearly $1.5 billion to get the equipment they need.

Some federal and state officials say that significant funding has been distributed, and more will be forthcoming as needs and the potential threats are assessed. They also acknowledge that there are growing and competing demands for government dollars at a time when many state and local governments are facing budget shortfalls.

"There's certainly room for additional funding, but given the funding that we do have, we just establish priorities and deal with the issues we feel are most critical," said Mr. Navarrete, the Arizona official. "I don't think we have any choice."

Their 9/11 Response: Be Prepared[2]

BY RICHARD T. COOPER
THE LOS ANGELES TIMES, SEPTEMBER 9, 2003

Kevin Clark is a second-generation cop, a street-tough police commander steeled in the cocaine wars of the South Bronx. Dan Hanfling is an Ivy League doctor. And Jim Schwartz spent his formative years answering fire alarms in suburbia.

Yet Clark, Hanfling and Schwartz have three things in common:

First, each was personally involved in responding to the terrorist attacks that struck the World Trade Center in New York and the Pentagon in Arlington, Va., on Sept. 11, 2001.

Second, each believes deep in his heart that such attacks will happen again. "I come to work every single day thinking today is going to be the day," Schwartz said recently.

Third, since Sept. 11, each has played a front-line role in the grass-roots struggle to get ready for next time—the nationwide effort to help local police, fire and emergency medical teams improve their readiness for new terrorist attacks or other mass catastrophes.

Working in the arena of first responders and local preparedness, they have seen the war on terrorism from the bottom up. And their experiences offer insight into why, despite measurable progress in many areas, the overall effort remains longer on plans and promises than on final results.

Clark, Hanfling and Schwartz, like local officials in towns and cities, state capitals and federal agencies across the country, have wrestled with tight budgets, red tape, politics and confusion—all the while driven by their memories of Sept. 11.

Clark, now police commissioner in Baltimore, is a native New Yorker and commanded the 44th Precinct in the Bronx two years ago. "When the first tower actually collapsed," he said, "it was like somebody put a sword right into your heart."

Schwartz was directing rescue efforts and the firefighting after a fuel-laden airliner smashed into the Defense Department's massive headquarters. He had to order police and firefighters to form a cordon and physically restrain military personnel from rushing back into the building to search for comrades. Minutes later, a huge section of the structure collapsed into flaming rubble.

"Many of them suddenly faced the reality that if we hadn't given that order, they'd have been dead," Schwartz said.

---

2. Article by Richard T. Cooper from *The Los Angeles Times* September 9, 2003. Copyright © *The Los Angeles Times*. Reprinted with permission.

Hanfling, as head of emergency management for the largest hospital system in Washington's Virginia suburbs, put emergency rooms on alert for the expected flood of trauma cases.

Hours later, as medical director of one of the first search and rescue teams to penetrate the Pentagon's shattered interior, he received the news that no one inside was likely to be alive. There was nothing left to do but tell his trauma teams to stand down.

Small wonder these three have played their roles since Sept. 11 with singular determination.

Life on the Street

If there are a million stories in the Naked City, as has been said of New York, then Kevin Clark probably heard the worst of them.

The son of a New York patrolman, Clark joined the force in 1981. He spent nine years in the South Bronx and three years in Spanish Harlem, "when the crack wars were in full effect."

On Sept. 11, 2001, Clark was driving to work across the George Washington Bridge and happened to glance downriver. To his astonishment, he saw the top of the trade center engulfed in a mushroom-shaped cloud.

When Clark called the NYPD operations center, a sergeant laconically informed him that they were sending a squad car to investigate. It was going to take more than that, Clark suggested.

At precinct headquarters, he said, "I told the radio dispatcher we weren't going to respond to anything except major crimes—robberies, murders, serious things," Clark said. "We just assumed it was an all-out attack on any symbols or infrastructure."

Last fall, when he accepted Mayor Martin O'Malley's invitation to come to Baltimore, Clark brought with him his wife, five children and two decades of experience fighting the drugs and violent crime that were ravaging Maryland's largest city.

He also brought a commitment to homeland security.

Supported by O'Malley, who has taken an aggressive stance on readiness, Clark has pushed hard for better equipment and organization. "It's a new world since 9/11, and police and fire and other first responders need new equipment like this," he said recently when the city announced that all 3,350 of its police officers would get biochemical masks and protective suits.

Such gains have been hard-won, however, and the police commissioner's frustration sometimes boils over.

"We're not prepared, whether people want to believe it or not," he said. "But everybody is playing politics, and it's with people's lives."

Part of the problem is that Baltimore, though it shows signs of revival after years of stagnation, is an old city with too many needs and too few resources.

And with almost all federal aid passing through the state, city officials say the Maryland Emergency Management Agency has been a bottleneck. A small agency that, until the war on terrorism, dealt mainly with natural disasters, it was not prepared for its new burdens.

The $1.15 million worth of biochemical protective gear for the police is a case in point.

Originally, the emergency agency sought to standardize first responder gear throughout the state and make itself the central purchasing agent. "Interoperability" is generally considered a good thing.

But the agency went so far as to specify models of equipment, Clark said, and it created a purchase list that betrayed the state officials' lack of expertise.

In the case of biochemical gear, the agency approved only traditional gas masks. Clark wanted his officers to have a model that could use gas-mask filters but could also be converted to use air tanks—the same masks firefighters use.

[Dr.] Dan Hanfling says his biggest problem has been persuading homeland security officials to see hospitals as part of the first-response system.

Police would have to work alongside firefighters in a major disaster, city officials reasoned. They had memories of July 2001, when chemical tank cars derailed in a tunnel beneath the city and shut it down for four days.

Eventually, the state agreed to release federal funds for the more advanced units. The breakthrough is a morale booster for officers, who had felt their safety was being ignored, Clark said. The only problem is, it will be a year or more before all the funds come through, the equipment is delivered and the whole department is trained to use it.

"If we started on our own goal line Sept. 11," O'Malley said, "we're probably up to the 20- or 30-yard line now."

Outside the Circle?

Absurd as it may sound, Dan Hanfling says his biggest problem has been persuading homeland security officials to see hospitals as part of the first-response system.

It's not that anyone thinks hospitals aren't part of that system, he said. It's that many officials make an unconscious assumption that, when disaster strikes, the hospitals will be ready. As a result, preparedness programs have tended to focus on bolstering police, fire and emergency medical units.

"We needed to reset the focus of what is a first responder," Hanfling said. "Funding for hospital preparedness has been low and it has been slow."

For instance, last year the state of Virginia received $23 million from the federal Health Resources Service Administration. The state health department took $20 million. The remaining $2.8 million was divided evenly among the state's six administrative regions.

Northern Virginia, home to the Pentagon, the CIA, two important Army posts and a plethora of other federal installations, as well as Reagan National Airport and hundreds of thousands of residents, got $383,000.

While growing up in New York and going to medical school at Brown University in Rhode Island, Hanfling never thought he would end up in disaster medicine, much less that terrorist attacks on the trade center and Pentagon would launch him on a crusade.

Almost every Sunday when he was a boy, he and his family traveled down the west side of Manhattan to have dinner with his paternal grandfather in Flatbush.

Hanfling began to notice a huge hole being dug east of the elevated highway. "What's that?" he asked his mother.

"They're building the world's tallest buildings," she replied.

Two years ago, he visited colleagues working at ground zero. "In my mind, I flashed back 35 years," he said. "I was seeing the exact same thing I was seeing as a child—a gigantic hole in the ground."

Hanfling wears multiple hats in the field of disaster medicine, in addition to his work for the INOVA Fairfax hospital system and the highly regarded Fairfax County Urban Search and Rescue team.

So he had a bird's-eye view of what went wrong in the Washington, D.C., area on Sept. 11, and of what's happened since.

For example, although INOVA's huge Fairfax hospital is the designated Class I trauma center for northern Virginia, and it dispatched its two helicopters to the Pentagon, none of the injured was sent to Fairfax.

For complicated reasons, the injured were scattered among other hospitals, some of them overburdened and less well-equipped for severe traumas.

After the terrorist attacks, Hanfling took a leading role in a campaign to make the system better. He helped organize all metropolitan hospitals into an alliance committed to common goals. Another organization was started for the whole emergency-response community.

The groups gave members a stronger political voice. They also made it easier for the organizations, which are spread over two states and the District of Columbia, to work together. "Prior to Sept. 11, the Potomac River was more like the Potomac Ocean," Hanfling said.

One result: A public-private partnership has put together a new radio network that ties all area hospitals together to share information about patient loads, emergency room status and other data. Previously, the hospitals relied on a shaky system of faxes and phone calls.

Gospel of Togetherness

Among first responders, none had a more comprehensive view of the attack on the Pentagon than Jim Schwartz. And he came away from that experience preaching a gospel that sets him apart from many involved in emergency management.

"I don't think money is the answer to all our problems," he says.

Schwartz believes that it is more important to develop regional programs that knit neighboring police, fire, emergency management services and public health units into teams. Sharing common procedures, holding joint exercises and developing trust among senior officials before trouble strikes, he says, will enable disparate organizations to function almost as one.

> *"I don't think money is the answer to all our problems."*—Jim Schwartz, Arlington County Fire Department

---

The approach can improve effectiveness, he says, and save money.

"Every community in the country doesn't need a bomb team, but every community in the country needs to know where it is going to get a bomb team," he said by way of illustration.

Schwartz believes the virtue of approaching emergency response on a regional basis was demonstrated at the Pentagon on Sept. 11. "All the work we had done prior to 9/11 is what made it possible," he said.

It was decades in the making.

Growing up in a semirural southeastern suburb of Washington, Jim Schwartz wanted to be a fireman. And when he joined the full-time Arlington County Fire Department, he said, he thought he would "spend 20 years riding a truck, going to building fires and medical emergencies."

He did all that, but Schwartz's abilities turned out to extend beyond the back of a single firetruck. As a lieutenant, captain, battalion chief and assistant fire chief for operations, he played a role in bringing about a remarkable transformation: Although Washington's northern Virginia suburbs are divided into half a dozen independent municipalities, the fire departments serving the largest of them have integrated their operations to a rare degree.

Going beyond "mutual aid pacts," Arlington, Fairfax County and the city of Alexandria intertwined their independent fire departments so completely that today, when alarms come in, dispatchers send the nearest equipment.

In Schwartz's view, that compatibility made all the difference two years ago.

Alerted by a call from Arlington Engine 101, which was returning from a training exercise and radioed that it was "watching a plane go down," Schwartz was at the scene within five minutes.

What he and others found transcended their experience and their imaginations. Dead and wounded were strewn over the lawn. Thousands of workers streamed from the building.

Yet operations unfolded with remarkable smoothness. As fire, police and rescue units arrived, most knew their roles and how to plug into the command and communications systems.

It may have looked like chaos, but it resulted in a remarkable fact, Schwartz said: "Ninety-four people were sent to hospitals from the Pentagon that morning. And only one of them subsequently died of their injuries."

Two years later, while money for better equipment and training is needed almost everywhere, what is needed more, Schwartz believes, is the local political will to create that kind of teamwork.

Are State and Local "First Responders" Getting the Federal Funding They Say They Need?[3]

By David Clarke
CQ Weekly, June 14, 2003

"We have a saying inside our department," Homeland Security Secretary Tom Ridge said recently. "The homeland will be secure when the hometowns are secure."

It's a nice turn of a phrase, but homilies do not pay the bills, and if anything has drowned out Ridge's avuncular assurances over the past year, it is the incessant cries of state and local authorities for more money to make their hometowns secure.

"I think it will come up again and again, and in spades, if there is another attack," said New Haven, Conn., Mayor John DeStefano Jr., who is also president of the National League of Cities.

If rescue units ever again race to smoking ruins comparable to the World Trade Center, indeed there probably will not be much debating over first responder spending. But until then, Washington and local governments will continue to wrangle over not just how much the federal government will provide, but who should distribute the funding and how to rejigger grant "formulas."

When President Bush on June 6, 2002, announced his support for a Department of Homeland Security, the political landscape in Washington shook like an earthquake. But the foundation for many of the state and local issues that have preoccupied homeland officials, members of Congress, governors and mayors since then arrived a few months before—on Feb. 4, 2002, when Bush unveiled his fiscal 2003 budget request.

At the time, Congress had appropriated $1 billion for first responders for fiscal 2002. Now, Bush was proposing that $3.5 billion in counterterrorism grants be made available to state and local programs for training and equipping firefighters, police officers and other emergency crews—all of which would be lumped together as "first responders." He also wanted the grants managed solely by the Federal Emergency Management Agency (FEMA).

Consolidating these programs under FEMA was an idea the administration floated the year before, but this first post-Sept. 11 budget proposal gave the White House the opportunity to really push it onto the agenda.

On its face, the idea of consolidating the programs in FEMA was logical. But the president's shift would have required the Justice Department, whose Office for Domestic Preparedness (ODP) handled a lot of this territory, and the members of Congress who authorize and appropriate its funding, to cede some control. It also would have called for local police officials to deal with an agency that had no law enforcement responsibilities or experience, another thing they were not eager to embrace.

But what really irritated state and local officials was the idea that almost all of the $3.5 billion in counterterrorism funding was not new money. In the same budget, the president proposed consolidating or eviscerating popular Clinton-era law enforcement grant programs, such as the Community Oriented Police Services (COPS) program.

To officials outside the Beltway it sounded like the administration was killing those programs to raise counterterrorist funds without really boosting the budget. The U.S. Conference of Mayors said such shifting and consolidation amounted to a nearly $800 million budget cut for programs.

"We must not rob Peter to pay Paul," New Orleans Mayor Marc Morial, then-president of the conference, said in March 2002. "We cannot afford to cut funding that helps prevent street crime in order to finance needed efforts to prevent terrorism."

The White House argued that COPS was a temporary program meant to help hire more police officers. And it insisted there was no proof that any of the other programs were actually contributing to the falling crime rate.

Rivals for Dollars

Adding to the roil was the reality that states and cities might well be united as a group in their pursuit of federal dollars, but they were rivals on the question of who should get them and how.

Local governments argued that funds should go directly to them because state bureaucracies would not only add more delay to the process, they would take sizable cuts off the top.

The states, which had an ally in Ridge, countered that sending money to them first would ensure that it was spent according to statewide plans that would help maximize dollars and avoid equipment duplication or incompatibilities, such as with radios.

The stage was set for a battle. Because Congress could not disentangle itself from election-year standoffs over spending and left for the year with 11 of its 13 annual appropriations bills on the shelf, the rhetoric only grew hotter.

Adding to the intensity was the fact that states and cities, which are almost all required to balance their budgets, have huge deficits hanging over them.

Homeland Security Money Finding Its Way to the States

Since the department opened in 2002, it has sent more than $2.2 billion to states and territories in grants from two agencies. The Office of Domestic Preparedness sends money— largely to police departments — for equipment, planning and training exercises. Emergency Management Performance grants go toward the same kind of programs for firefighters.

State grants:

(in millions of dollars)

State	ODP grant	EMP grant	Total
Alabama	$39.8	$5.2	$45.0
Alaska	21.0	2.8	23.8
Arizona	44.5	5.4	49.8
Arkansas	31.1	4.0	35.1
California	189.1	23.7	212.8
Colorado	39.8	4.9	44.7
Connecticut	34.8	4.6	39.4
Delaware	21.8	2.8	24.6
Florida	99.3	11.7	111.0
Georgia	59.6	7.3	66.8
Hawaii	23.9	3.2	27.2
Idaho	24.4	3.1	27.5
Illinois	79.5	9.4	88.9
Indiana	48.0	5.9	53.9
Iowa	32.2	4.1	36.3
Kansas	31.2	3.9	35.1
Kentucky	37.9	4.6	42.5
Louisiana	39.8	5.1	44.9
Maine	24.2	3.2	27.4
Maryland	44.5	5.4	49.9
Massachusetts	49.3	6.3	55.6
Michigan	67.0	8.5	75.5
Minnesota	42.4	5.2	47.6
Mississippi	31.9	4.0	36.0
Missouri	45.6	5.7	51.3
Montana	22.3	2.8	25.2
Nebraska	26.3	3.4	29.7
Nevada	28.4	3.5	31.9
New Hampshire	24.1	3.2	27.2
New Jersey	59.8	7.7	67.5
New Mexico	26.8	3.5	30.3
New York	111.6	13.8	125.4
North Carolina	58.5	7.3	65.8
North Dakota	21.0	2.7	23.7
Ohio	73.8	9.4	83.2
Oklahoma	35.0	4.4	39.3
Oregon	35.1	4.4	39.4
Pennsylvania	78.3	9.8	88.1
Rhode Island	23.1	3.1	26.2
South Carolina	37.9	4.9	42.9
South Dakota	21.6	2.6	24.2
Tennessee	46.2	5.7	51.9
Texas	124.0	14.8	138.8
Utah	29.2	3.7	32.9
Vermont	20.9	2.6	23.5
Virginia	53.5	6.7	60.2
Washington	47.5	5.8	53.2
West Virginia	26.7	3.2	29.9
Wisconsin	44.5	5.5	50.0
Wyoming	20.3	2.7	23.0

In February, Congress did not come close to quenching the thirst for more federal dollars when it finally appropriated $3.5 billion for first responders. That money was not all new, either. Appropriators chose to include programs such as COPS in their tally for the $3.5 billion, much to the consternation of state and local officials.

In April, members used the wartime supplemental bill (PL 108-11) to try to pacify some of those complaints by providing $4.3 billion for first responder, emergency planning and critical infrastructure protection programs.

As for who would get what when, Congress—with the administration's support—sided with the states but offered an olive branch to local officials: Money would go first to state capitals, but they would be required to "pass through" 80 percent of it to local governments.

As far as who would hand out the money, the law enforcement community and its congressional allies won out over the administration, which wanted the new department's Emergency Preparedness directorate to handle the grant programs once the law (PL 107-296) creating the Homeland Security Department was passed in November. Instead, the authority was given to ODP, which sits in Homeland's law enforcement wing, the Border and Transportation Security directorate.

But even this issue remains somewhat unresolved.

Ridge has announced his support for legislation (S 796) sponsored by Maine Republican and Senate Governmental Affairs Chairwoman Susan Collins that would move ODP up the organizational chart into the Office for State and Local Government Coordination, which reports directly to the secretary.

Now, dispersing money but wearing its green eyeshade, the department is turning a magnifying glass on the criteria, or "formula," it will use to award funding.

The formula passed by Congress in fall 2001 requires that about 35 percent to 40 percent of first responder funds be split equally among all states. ODP has distributed the rest based mostly on population.

But Ridge and many in Congress would like to tweak the formula so that while a state minimum would remain in place, the department could direct the rest by using criteria such as the likelihood that an area would be attacked and whether it had vulnerable sites such as nuclear or chemical plants nearby.

Collins has made revisiting the formula a top priority for her committee, while Congress set aside $100 million in the omnibus and $700 million in the supplemental spending bills for high-threat cities, such as New York and Washington.

Sending more money to those cities is again an idea few would dispute, but Ridge already has had to deal with questions from lawmakers about why cities in their states did not make the cut.

Still, the issue of redoing formulas and deciding which box on a chart will mail the checks may soon be relegated to a sideshow when Congress starts working on next year's spending bills and vectoring grants to cash-strapped hometowns.

"You're going to go where the game is being played," DeStefano said of this year's lobbying action. "And the game is going to be played in the appropriations bills."

Can We Talk?[4]

By Ellen Perlman
Governing, May 2003

The olive-drab, Navy-issue belt is stretched out across a table in a Washington, D.C., city building. It's a curiosity to behold: way too long and heavy for even a Sumo wrestler to use to hold up his pants. That's because it's hooked up with all manner of wireless devices, from cell phones to two-way pagers to personal digital assistants.

Suzanne Peck, the city's chief information officer, is on hand. She's explaining how the belt, which she hauls to seminars and conferences around town, represents how far the city's communications have come since 9/11, when the Pentagon was on fire, dial tones were not available and city officials from Mayor Anthony Williams on down were only able to get in touch with each other by typing e-mails or punching in text messages. In the aftermath of that crisis, district officials sat down to figure out what to do to improve their communications, to make sure they could talk rather than type during any future emergencies. What they came up with is on the belt: a battalion of communication devices and phone services. "Our strategy," Peck says, "is to give as many opportunities for alternate routing as possible."

The District of Columbia is not alone in grappling with shortcomings in interagency and inter-jurisdictional communications. With the heightened anxiety over terrorist threats, almost all state and local governments are struggling to attain an acceptable level of "homeland security." The daunting problems they face in getting there start with an inadequate definition of exactly what comprises homeland security and go on to an even more inadequate means of funding to get wherever it is they are supposed to go. Even within this imprecise and discomforting situation, however, there is evidence that, when it comes to their technology, a handful of governments are inching closer to building up an adequate security system.

What Do You Mean By That?

No one is quite sure how to spell out exactly what homeland security is. The federal definition is lofty, all-encompassing and discouragingly vague: "A concerted national effort to prevent terrorist attacks within the United States, reduce America's vulnerability to

---

The Big Picture

If money was no object and no political or institutional obstacles stood in the way, what would the ideal homeland security system look like? Here's the set-up that Tim Daniel, director of Missouri's Office of Homeland Security, envisions:

- In case of an incident, there is a complete situational awareness, from the governor's office on down to fire fighters on the scene.

- Regional organizations have good support from within their region and outside, with agencies from all over coming to the aid of each other.

- Smooth, interoperable communications systems enable police to talk to fire fighters, the FBI and emergency operations centers quickly and easily.

- Governments have biological, radiological and chemical detection capabilities deployed so they can detect a terrorist strike, down to a point in a building or a subway.

- People in locations considered to be at high risk for an attack—perhaps Manhattan or the Pentagon—wear detection devices that light up or sound off if biological agents are unleashed.

- Sophisticated, interoperable systems help prevent attacks. For instance, a system tracks ships and their cargo. Before a ship comes into port, officials know where it came from, what the ship is carrying, who is on board and where it's heading.

---

terrorism and minimize the damage and recover from attacks that do occur." That doesn't offer much in the way of a blueprint for action.

Nor does it suggest what does or does not fall within its boundaries. "There's hardly anything in the world that isn't affected by homeland security issues," says Harlin McEwen, chairman of the Communications and Technology Committee of the International Association of Chiefs of Police.

Money is an even bigger problem. Not much federal cash has been passed on to the states and localities to help fund responses—certainly not the $3.5 billion proposed by President Bush last January. New York and Washington, D.C.—the two cities that suffered most directly from 9/11—received some money early on. More recently, those two cities and five others—Chicago, Houston, Los Angeles, San Francisco and Seattle—were allotted a share of $100 million. The cities were chosen based on population density, critical infrastructure and vulnerability to attack.

Meanwhile, most localities, hesitant to make major investments in homeland security without federal money to defray costs, have had to spend their own funds on increased security. In a survey released in March, the U.S. Conference of Mayors reported that cities nationwide were spending about $70 million a week on additional homeland security measures due to the war with Iraq and the heightened level of threat alert. This is money on top of any funds they were already spending or planning to spend on post-9/11 homeland security. Mayors have been waiting for homeland secu-

Shopping List

If a government had millions of dollars to spend on securing technology for homeland security, what would it be able to buy?

Washington, D.C., is one place to look. It received $159 million for homeland security from the federal government in the aftermath of 9/11. The city is planning to plow $45 million of it into technology that will help make it a safer place.

The project list includes:

- Building an emergency preparedness Intranet system and securing the Internet perimeter of the city against virus and hacker intrusion.

- Enhancing a public safety radio system. Radios have been known to fail when law enforcement officers are in a Metro train tunnel or behind the walls of a thick concrete building. Fixing the faulty radio system had long been on the District's to-do list, and the infusion of federal homeland security dollars means it will get done faster.

- In addition, the District will use its own funds to build a 150,000-square-foot unified command center. The purpose of that facility is to "facilitate communications at whatever level necessary," says Suzanne Peck, the District's chief information officer.

rity funds for more than 18 months, says Baltimore Mayor Martin O'Malley, who chairs the Conference's Homeland Security Task Force. "Cities," he says, "urgently need direct, flexible financial assistance to meet their homeland security needs."

This is not a view that falls with favor on federal ears. Rather, Howard Schmidt, a special adviser to the president, suggests that state and local governments shouldn't be playing the waiting game, that good managers move forward with what they've got, "in the true American spirit to help themselves."

State and local governments may not be thrilled to hear that they are expected to do a lot with very little, yet they have to move forward. Technology and security officials have to make sure they are protecting government networks from cyber attacks. They must also tend to all the technologies that play a part in emergency services, disaster recovery and response—from GIS mapping to criminal justice databases to wireless communications systems. And, of course, public officials and law enforcement personnel have to figure out how to "talk" to one another during the first critical moments of an incident.

At the same time, governments are not starting from scratch. Many have pieces already in place for homeland security. They're the protocols and systems that come into play at times of natural disasters and for crime prevention. What has changed is the 9/11 mindset: the recognition that those plans and systems need to be upgraded and reinforced to protect against the threat of widespread and devastating attacks that most people never would have contemplated before 9/11.

Strong Signals

Lack of money isn't the only complaint about federal input on homeland security. State and local agencies are clamoring for guidance, but the federal Homeland Security Department is in a period of organization: It is still figuring out how to run its own operations as a new agency and absorb personnel from nearly two dozen federal agencies. Not surprisingly, it hasn't come up with much guidance or coordination for state and local efforts.

Communications interoperability is a case in point. The ability for various emergency agencies to talk to each other at a time of crisis has become the top "homeland security" priority for many local governments. Too many emergency workers use outdated and incompatible systems that hinder their ability to share critical information in the midst of a crisis.

This is not news to Randy Bruegman, fire chief of Clackamas County District One in Oregon, and president of the International Association of Fire Chiefs. By way of background to the problem, Bruegman talks about a recent incident: Fire personnel in Clackamas responded to a shooting, as did police and medical units. The radio system of the police in charge of the situation used a different frequency than the fire and medic units on the scene. The fire fighters had to resort to charades to inform medical personnel. "We were doing hand signals back and forth to let them know there was a shooting and medical help was needed," Bruegman says. "That sounds fairly far-fetched, but it happens every day. You drive five miles and fire departments can't talk to fire departments, police can't talk to police." It's a frustrating reality that hinders emergency work—and that's just for routine events.

Bruegman is looking to the Department of Homeland Security to articulate a national plan on what local responders need to do and how they should do it. If there is no such plan, departments likely will continue to replace what they have with new equipment that still will not be able to communicate with others. If there were a plan with standards, departments could move in a direction that gets them on the same wavelength eventually. "The worst thing we can do from a local and national perspective," he says, "is spend billions of dollars and find that the equipment and response is not interoperable."

Interoperability imposes an enormous task. There are many different issues to address. For instance, on the communications front, there isn't enough radio spectrum available for all public safety agencies to be on the same frequency, a situation that hampers interoperability. But it's very a complex issue that requires congressional and Federal Communications Commission decisions on who is using what spectrum. A resolution might require an overhaul of the system that would include private users swapping spectrum with public users, a complicated and expensive proposition. And that's just one issue on the table.

Still, instead of getting "analysis paralysis," local agencies should be taking steps now to get prepared for the unknown, Bruegman says. That includes making sure there are local plans for all "target" areas, such as schools; that all responding personnel are fully trained; that local police and FBI departments sit down and share information; that plans are in place on how to collectively command a situation when different units respond to an incident. If radios don't communicate, people still can figure out a system using pagers or cell phones or whatever else is available. "It doesn't cost a lot of money," he says. "It's an attitude change. We have to commit to working collectively with other agencies, whether local, state or federal."

George Ake, who works on a regional wireless interoperability project in the D.C.-Maryland-Virginia metro area, supports that notion. Where Suzanne Peck carries around a belt hung with devices, Ake takes a more metaphorical approach. He shows a slide of three little girls playing in a sandbox. He tells audiences where he speaks that government agencies will benefit from sharing their ideas and their toys. "Most of the time people don't play well together," he says.

Chicago area law enforcement agencies have gotten much better at playing together. More than 130 state, local and federal law enforcement agencies in the area have taken it upon themselves to share the job of collecting, analyzing and disseminating information to one another to thwart criminals and terrorists. They're all tied into the same database for this enterprise project. "We're collecting a lot of information we historically collected on paper, so we can analyze it in real time," says Ron Huberman, assistant deputy superintendent of the Chicago Police Department.

> *"We have to commit to working collectively with other agencies, whether local, state or federal."*
> —Randy Bruegman, an Oregon fire chief

Work on the interoperable system started at least a year before September 11, 2001. The Chicago police department developed the system, and some agencies that had no system of their own adopted it. Other agencies are sharing information by maintaining two systems, and still others are migrating over to the enterprise system from their own. With all those departments working side by side, the system has become a management tool that can determine crime trends and look at strategies criminals deployed. Departments can put together details from multiple crimes and find patterns using a data warehouse analysis.

Networking

New York State is reaching beyond its borders for help in detecting patterns of terrorist or criminal behavior. The state has created an Information Sharing and Analysis Center, or ISAC, a way to share and analyze information and give timely warnings of cyber or physical attacks to 13 participating states. If, for instance, Florida employees were to see a virus on their networks, they would immediately alert the other members about what they were experiencing, using 24/7 contact information that has been gathered for the purpose. If similar problems were happening in, say, three other states, they'd know what they were seeing was not an isolated incident but a widespread problem.

It is not particularly the habit of IT staff to spread the word about their networks being infiltrated. The first reaction often has been to keep it quiet and work to get it fixed before anyone knows about it. "Sharing information about being breached was so difficult before," says Will Pelgrin, director of New York's Office of Cyber Security and Critical Infrastructure Coordination. "A staff person who found it was always trying to correct it before the boss ever learned about it." However, in these times of purposeful attacks, officials are stressing that sharing information is important and that it's best for others to know what was vulnerable so that everyone else is less vulnerable.

The state did what it considered a successful practice run of its procedures on President's Day weekend in February. All states checked in about what they were seeing on their networks, which happened to be nothing damaging on those days. But like a fire drill, the states got to make a dry run of what they'd do if they were seeing a cyber attack. "I can't just protect my own network," says Pelgrin, who hopes eventually all 50 states will join the ISAC. "There are too many dependencies with other agencies. It has to be a collaborative effort."

The Washington, D.C., area knows about collaboration. Long before 9/11, Maryland, Virginia and District of Columbia first responders found themselves having to communicate during several harrowing situations. Most of the time, that communication was fragmented.

In 1999, the region began working on the Capital Wireless Integrated Network or CapWIN project, a wireless interoperability project that is using the resources of three states, several local governments and the federal government. For this project, the governments are not focusing on getting radios to talk to one another. Instead, they are using a Web browser that first responders will have on their mobile computers, personal digital assistants or data-enabled mobile phones. Those with existing mobile data systems will go through an electronic bridge to get connected to other systems they couldn't communicate with before. (Those without mobile computers, such as the Maryland State Police, will be getting them.)

The Alexandria, Virginia, police department, for instance, has a good mobile data system for its force. But it can't connect with neighboring jurisdictions. In a few months, if all goes well, the Alexandria system will be able to communicate with the rest of the systems in the region, via a set of computers housed in Greenbelt, Maryland. Essentially what's happening is that equipment in Greenbelt is being used as a gateway to "translate French into German," says George Ake, the project coordinator. That is, Alexandria-speak is being translated into other neighboring government-speak without any of those governments having to buy new systems. The software is off the shelf and standards-based. "People can't afford to buy new systems," Ake says. "If they already spent millions for a new system, they're not going to be really happy throwing it out and starting all over again."

When there is a disaster that requires the cooperation of police, fire and medical units, first responders will be able to sit in their various vehicles or offices and log on to a computer chat room to discuss who should do what next. Or they can use instant messaging. They will get information from the FBI or a transportation department or a criminal database. The first governments had been expected to start using the system in March but that was delayed and they anticipate having the system ready for use within the next few weeks.

Double Whammy

While homeland security may be a new term that will foster a new thinking process, the equipment that is purchased and the partnerships formed can serve a dual purpose, and "regular" investments can do double duty for homeland security. Virginia area fire fighters and emergency medical technicians, for instance, might tap into the CapWIN wireless interoperability system when a truck with hazardous materials turns over on the Capital Beltway. Cook County, Illinois, is doing an aerial flyover for its GIS system that will provide location information that can be used for crime, natural disasters or terrorism-related incidents.

While interoperability is useful, the ability to communicate from system to system presents a fundamental challenge for any technology environment. The tools exist to connect up those who want to be connected, but connectivity can mean the opposite of security. A connected system becomes only as strong as its weakest link. The more hands and eyes on data, from various departments with different levels of management and differing policies on protecting data, the more the risk level rises. The result, says Kirk Bailey, Seattle's CIO, is a "never ending litany of potential liability."

Most operating systems were developed without security in mind, so enabling them to speak to one another creates additional risks. And that problem, Bailey suggests, is almost unsolvable.

That doesn't mean that governments should back off from their goal of sharing information. What's needed is a business and technology evaluation on how much risk to take, and that's not a new concept. Federal regulations for the banking industry and health regulations under HIPAA—the health care privacy law that mandates electronic transfer of information—speak to standards and rules on privacy and security. At the same time, state and local agencies are looking for the most affordable, best bang for the buck option. "The information age has wrought upon us a unique challenge," Bailey says. "It's very hard to do."

Pounds of Cure[5]

By Kim A. O'Connell
American City & County, June 2003

The anthrax attacks of fall 2001 forced most U.S. citizens to realize how bioterrorism could endanger them right where they live. Since then, federal, state and local public health agencies have worked to prepare for bioterrorism and other large-scale public health threats. On a national level, the Washington, D.C.-based Department of Health and Human Services—the lead federal agency on threats to public health—has established a Bioterrorism Command Center. The center is equipped with population- and weather-mapping systems, as well as with the ability to track public health crises nationwide, so that local governments can be alerted quickly to possible threats.

Locally, governments are generally less prepared. According to the Washington, D.C.-based National Association of County and City Health Officials (NACCHO), many large local health agencies have invested a great deal of time and effort to prepare for bioterrorism. However, most local governments still lack the resources to develop their threat-identification-and-response capacity, hindering their ability to keep residents safe.

Bioterrorism is just one of the many public health emergencies that local governments must anticipate. Other threats include strange and unexpected diseases, such as severe acute respiratory syndrome (SARS). Furthermore, governments always must be ready for outbreaks of more conventional public health threats, such as influenza.

"Even before Sept. 11, and clearly following [the attacks] and the anthrax scare, the importance of public health as an element of community response to acts of terrorism has grown," says NACCHO President Patrick Libbey. "Part of being prepared is having in place a functional public health response capacity and not just [in response to] a terrorist event. SARS is another example of how quickly a local government needs to respond."

NACCHO has identified five areas that local governments should improve to prepare for possible public health emergencies. Those are preparedness planning and readiness assessment; surveillance and epidemiology capacity; health alert networks, communications and information technology; risk communication and health information dissemination; and education and training.

"In this country, [regarding] our public health capacity and infrastructure, we've let it go," Libbey says. "We aren't going to make up decades of neglect in one year of federal funding." However, Libbey admits that homeland security funding is making a difference, slowly. "We are better prepared now than we were a year ago," he says. "But we have a ways to go if you define preparedness as having fully developed plans in place."

Areas of Concern

In 1999, NACCHO developed the Local Centers for Public Health Preparedness project, in which the Atlanta-based Centers for Disease Control and Prevention provided funding for three local health agencies—DeKalb County, Ga.; Denver; and Monroe County, N.Y.— to conduct bioterrorism training and improve their readiness. Recently, a fourth agency, the Kansas City, Mo., Health Department, signed on as well. Already, their efforts have served as models for information-sharing and training on bioterrorism preparedness—as more and more local governments factor public health into their homeland security plans.

DeKalb County, for example, has developed a bioterrorism response plan and related educational exercises. The plan consists of several sections, including an overview of federal agencies and their responsibilities, reference material and local response agencies' roles. The plan is available on CD-ROM for use by other local public health agencies. Related educational exercises take emergency response personnel and hospital staff through the likely progression of a bioterrorism event, using botulism, plague and smallpox as possible scenarios.

"It can be difficult to get a first response team to understand that a bioterrorism event is very different [from other emergency events]," says William Dyal, director of population-based services for the DeKalb County Board of Health. "There may not be a site to go to or a place to put yellow tape around. The primary response isn't an immediate, on-the-scene response." More often, Dyal says, the response unfolds over time, as people get sick and a pattern emerges.

Dyal adds that emergency response workers commonly want to lump biological and chemical threats together, but he points out that the two types of terrorism would play out very differently and require different responses. A chemical attack, for example, would always produce an actual scene where people are falling ill very quickly, Dyal says. Biological attacks unfold more slowly and often mysteriously.

Another crucial element of preparedness and prevention is surveillance. "How well is your public health system monitoring health conditions in your community? How 'real time' is your data?" Libbey asks. "Much of our surveillance has been passive. What we need is much more active surveillance that identifies, closer to real time, changes in health conditions."

Basic surveillance capacities would work just as well to identify an outbreak of SARS, smallpox or West Nile virus, Libbey says. After implementing a basic monitoring capacity, communities can start to tailor their surveillance to specific conditions. "You would up your West Nile surveillance as mosquito season approaches," Libbey cites as an example. "You have to have a more active, more robust way of gathering that information in a systematic way."

Lines of Communication

As in all emergency response plans, communication among pertinent parties is paramount. That is especially true in a public health situation, where emergency responders may not have as thorough an understanding of a viral outbreak, for instance, as they might have dealing with an explosion.

"Most of what [emergency responders] deal with has been event-specific—things that go boom," Libbey says. "Now we're looking at conditions that will roll out less specifically, that are less event-based. We're doing a lot of work engaging [the Federal Emer-

---

As in all emergency response plans, communication among pertinent parties is paramount.

---

gency Management Agency] FEMA in teaching public health workers incident command for working under these conditions. But if you're just introducing each other and exchanging information for the first time during an event, it's not going to go well."

Understanding the broad spectrum of involved parties helps. Libbey cites the anthrax attacks, for example, which had a criminal element and involved law enforcement. With SARS affecting tourism in certain places, economic and business entities might be stakeholders as well.

Technological interoperability for communication also is an increasingly understood concept that DeKalb County and many others are working to improve. DeKalb, for one, has outfitted key public health personnel with police radios; if a warning comes through, public health workers then tap into a cellular telephone network to reach key parties.

Education and training are as important as planning, surveillance and communication. "One of the things that is last to be funded and first to go is the notion of training and exercise," Libbey says. "At least in public health, and I suspect in other disciplines, it's typically underfunded and it's usually something you do on top of an already full plate. But in emergency preparedness, it's an ongoing need."

A Regional Approach

In addition to improving communication and education in a single locality, bioterrorism preparedness also requires local governments to develop response plans regionally. "There was a time in local governments when regional was not a good word," Libbey says. But that has changed since Sept. 11, Libbey adds.

Washington [state], for example, has taken the lead in encouraging its local governments to work together. County public health departments are divided into regions, with one county—usually the most populated—taking the lead. For example, Thurston County is the lead in a western Washington region that also includes the Grays Harbor, Lewis, Mason and Pacific counties.

The county recently has developed a bioterrorism response plan and provided some related training. For instance, the region has trained staff from all the counties' hospitals on smallpox outbreaks, providing voluntary vaccinations as part of the training. Even if public health workers did not want to get vaccinated, they were trained on what to do if an outbreak occurred.

Of particular importance to the region is the applicability of the bioterrorism response plan in other public health scenarios. "What we're trying to do is make sure that whatever we do has life well beyond an event," says Sherri McDonald, director of the Thurston County Public Health and Social Services Department. The smallpox plan, for example, dealt with how to administer vaccinations to many people at one time—a plan that could apply to the distribution of antibiotics in a bioterrorism event, McDonald says.

"We're trying to get the message out to the general public that the kinds of things they would do to prepare for a bioterrorism attack [such as stockpiling first aid and other supplies] might help them in other ways, such as for a flood or a winter storm," McDonald says.

Preparing for the Future

Looking ahead, NACCHO has piloted a voluntary certification program for local health departments called Public Health Ready. Certification would demonstrate that a local health organization has a response plan in place, that the plan has been exercised with community partners and that the organization has identified subsequent steps.

The certification program encourages local governments to identify the steps they can take to protect residents. "It's not feasible or appropriate that every local health department be at the same level of readiness," Libbey says. "But they have to understand their level of readiness and know how to access that level of readiness."

Perhaps most important, public health agencies need to maintain communication with other emergency personnel. In the absence of an actual attack, local departments can easily become complacent. "The response plan is only as good as your relationship with the first-response community," Dyal says.

III.
Intelligence Gathering
and Civil Liberties

Editors' Introduction

The more the 9/11 attacks are investigated, the clearer it seems that American intelligence services failed in their primary purpose: to monitor and deter the nation's enemies. There were three major intelligence agencies operating in and out of the United States before 9/11—the Federal Bureau of Investigation (FBI), the Central Intelligence Agency (CIA), and the National Security Agency (NSA)—as well as smaller units under the armed services. Not one seems to have guessed what was coming. The warning signals that did reach headquarters seemed so far-fetched—requiring such a stretch of the imagination—that they were never treated with the urgency they deserved, while vital information got old, cold, and lost in the shuffle. Needless to say, the intelligence community has been under fire ever since, and there are now more agencies than ever.

In "Could It Happen Again?" from *Time* magazine, Michael Duffy analyzes the failures of U.S. intelligence with regard to 9/11 and the steps that have been taken since to ensure that history does not repeat itself. In fairness to the intelligence services, he points out that they have been starved of funds and personnel since the end of the Cold War, and that clues to Al Qaeda's designs were hardly lying around in plain sight. However, he believes the clues were there—he lists several—and that inspired detective work might have prevented the attacks. On a "report card" that includes such items as establishing a central information clearinghouse and hiring more Arab-language specialists, Duffy gives the intelligence services some B's and C's, but a lot of "incompletes."

In "Mission Impossible?" from the *IEEE Spectrum*, Jean Kumagai describes the plight of the FBI, the nation's premier law enforcement agency. It must continue to investigate crimes and gather evidence for prosecutors to use in court but at the same time play a greatly expanded role in counterterrorism—investigating crimes before they can happen. This will require a very different mindset from the old, reliable G-man's "make the case" approach. Besides radically different training, agents of the new FBI will also need better computer programs to access the Bureau's sprawling files and better equipment to communicate with each other.

James Bond notwithstanding, most intelligence work consists of unglamorous toil: gathering and interpreting information. Quite a lot of information about individuals is stored in the files of public agencies (health, motor vehicle, military, and police) and in records kept by banks, credit card companies, merchants, and the like. In "Digging Through Data for Omens" from *U.S. News & World Report*, Dana Hawkins discusses the utility of "data mining" these records—using computers to search the material for patterns in personal history, travel, and spending that might indicate terrorist activity. Data-mining techniques are already employed by private industry to target potential customers and to protect against fraud, but the counterterrorism effort would widen the net and raise the stakes considerably, a prospect that alarms many civil libertarians. Surveillance technology is a particular concern of Gene Stephens's in "Can We Be Safe *and* Free?" reprinted from *USA Today* magazine and subtitled, "The Dilemma Terrorism Creates." Stephens explores the point at which surveillance for security purposes shades into social control; then, drawing on what he knows of research in progress, he imagines a nightmarish future in which each successive technological advance takes another bite out of liberty and perfect safety is achieved by eliminating human choice altogether. America might have a better future, he suggests, if the nation were less preoccupied with techno-feats and more attentive to the poverty and despair that seem to engender terrorism.

Finally, in two articles selected from a series in the online magazine *Slate*, Dahlia Lithwick and Julia Turner examine some of the more controversial provisions of the USA PATRIOT Act. The acronym stands for "United and Strengthening America by Providing Appropriate Tools Required to Intercept and Obstruct Terrorism." Passed right after 9/11, the act was intended to speed the "war on terror" by making it easier for law enforcement to conduct searches, tap telephones, arrest people, and so forth. PATRIOT sailed through Congress in 2001 but has since come under attack, partly because Congress has learned that the special provisions of the act have been invoked in quite a number of cases that had nothing to do with terrorism. Lithwick and Turner survey the law and the furor that surrounds it and advise readers to review the act themselves. (A Web address to the complete text of the PATRIOT Act is included in the list of Web sites in the "Bibliography" at the end of this book.) Since the measures taken to fight terrorism may well outlast the threat itself, this sounds like good advice.

Could It Happen Again?[1]

By Michael Duffy
Time, August 4, 2003

Looking back on it now, it is difficult to choose the precise moment when U.S. government officials—hobbled by old-fashioned rules, saddled with ancient computers that could not talk to one another and riven by silly bureaucratic rivalries—missed their best chance to thwart the plot by 19 hijackers to take over four airplanes, turn them into flying missiles and kill almost 3,000 people nearly two years ago.

Was it in early 1999, when the National Security Agency, eavesdropping on a suspected terrorist facility in the Middle East, first learned (but kept to itself) that a 25-year-old Saudi named Nawaf Alhazmi had links to Osama bin Laden? Or was it in March 2000, when the CIA heard from its spies overseas (but did not tell the FBI) that Alhazmi had flown to Los Angeles a few weeks before? Then there was the bungled meeting between the CIA and the FBI in June 2001, when the CIA hinted at Alhazmi's role but would not put everything it knew on the table. Washington may have had one more chance to change history in late August 2001, when FBI headquarters finally heard that Alhazmi and other bin Laden operatives were loose in the U.S. But against the advice of detectives in the field, agents at FBI headquarters assigned the case a low priority, and nearly two weeks passed before the bureau asked its Los Angeles field office to track down the suspects. That last e-mail was dated Sept. 11, 2001.

All summer long, the normally rarefied issue of secret intelligence—the good and bad, the lost and found—has preoccupied Washington and perplexed the nation. Before Sept. 11, the government was unable or unready to connect the dots left by a growing army of terrorists bent on killing thousands of Americans. More recently, the government has appeared to be a little too ready to connect dots that may not have been there at all—that is, the prewar case for Iraq's weapons of mass destruction. Two years ago, the bar for proving a danger to our security was set too high; two years later, partly because of what happened on Sept. 11, the bar has seemed a bit too low. How do we get it right?

In the terrifying days that followed the attacks of 2001, when very little was comforting, it was almost a relief to hear top Bush Administration officials argue that there was really no way the U.S. government could have foreseen, much less prevented, the

---

deadly attacks on Washington and New York City. Osama bin Laden's plot was too diabolical, they said, too well executed and too perfectly aimed at the blind spots of our homeland defense for anyone to have imagined or foiled it. "We were surprised by what happened here," said Vice President Dick Cheney five days afterward.

But it is now clear that the real story is much more unsettling. The blunt conclusion of the bipartisan House and Senate joint inquiry into the causes of 9/11, released last week, was that while no one in the government "identified the time, place and specific nature of the attacks," the government lost repeated opportunities to detect, if not disrupt, the hijackers in 2000 and 2001.

It would not have been easy, and piecing it all together would have required resourcefulness, brilliance and more than a little luck. But it was possible. The question now is not so much, How did it happen?—every school kid knows that story—but, What has been done in the two years since 9/11 to prevent it from happening again? What steps has the government taken so that the gathering of intelligence and the profitable use of it is assured and routine? With the

---

The government lost repeated opportunities to detect, if not disrupt, the hijackers in 2000 and 2001.

---

joint report as a guide, we have analyzed six critical problems with America's intelligence posture and compiled a progress report on what has been done to fix them in the past two years.

Making Terrorism the Focus: A central problem before 9/11 was that neither the Clinton nor the Bush team had a clear, well-defined strategy for fighting terrorism. It just wasn't a priority. Clinton finished his second term focused on securing a Middle East peace, and Bush came into office thinking more about Beijing and Moscow than Afghanistan. And to the extent that either team focused on terrorism, both believed that the chief threat was to U.S. troops overseas, not everyday civilians at home. Those who did worry about Al Qaeda often worried alone. In December 1998, CIA Director George Tenet told his lieutenants, "We are at war. I want no resources or people spared in this effort, either inside the CIA or the community." But there is little evidence that Tenet shared this declaration with other government agencies. At the National Security Council, top terrorist hunter Richard Clarke was also on a quest to adopt an all-out action plan against bin Laden, and in 2001 he urged the new Administration to do so. But the Bush team slow-walked its strategy through an interagency review for seven months.

After 9/11, Bush reorganized his entire presidency around the war on terrorism, and he has not looked back. He has launched two wars, sent special-forces teams to at least half a dozen other coun-

---

Intelligence Report Card

Problem: Obsessed with secrecy and drowning in data, the NSA, the CIA and the FBI failed to share information about the 9/11 hijackers.

What Was Proposed: A single government-wide clearinghouse for faster distribution of informants' tips and terrorist threats.

How They're Doing: The Terrorist Threat Integration Center opened in April—and there's still some confusion about who is actually in charge. Too soon to tell.

Problem: The CIA lacked spies inside terrorist cells and had been unable to penetrate Osama bin Laden's inner circle.

What Was Proposed: The CIA would revive its original emphasis on human sources, and CIA paramilitary units and Pentagon special-ops troops would conduct joint operations.

How They're Doing: Spooks and troops fight side by side in Iraq and Afghanistan; the CIA's Operations Directorate is out recruiting.

Problem: The FBI was slow to hunt down bin Laden operatives and dismissed field agents' hunches about their activities at American flight schools.

What Was Proposed: Quietly replace much of the bureau's aging management; install state-of-the-art computers; change the reactive G-man culture and teach agents to look around corners.

How They're Doing: Progress is slow. Some agents got e-mail only this year.

Problem: Many of the agencies had too few analysts and translators; not many spoke the dialects used by Al Qaeda; analysts from the eavesdropping National Security Agency (NSA) hadn't finished digesting all the intercepts from 1999.

What Was Proposed: Hired hundreds of analysts and linguists to track terrorists.

How They're Doing: Some success in reducing the backlog at NSA; Arabic speakers at the FBI have nearly tripled since 9/11, to 208.

---

tries, pumped billions into old spy networks and new unmanned weapons, and engineered the biggest reorganization of government since the cold war by creating the Department of Homeland Security. At home, he has signed legislation granting sweeping new powers to the Justice Department and other law-enforcement agencies. Overseas, he has authorized a new military doctrine that abandons deterrence for pre-emptive action. The government has focused on these threats in unprecedented ways. As Bush said last week, "We are slowly but surely dismantling the Al Qaeda network."

Stopping the Stovepiping: Apart from the terrorists, the biggest enemy the government faced before 9/11 was itself. Agents at both the FBI and the CIA had a longtime habit of stovepiping—keeping information to themselves or sharing it with only a handful of people. That made for good secret-keeping but discouraged critical thinking by the people on the front lines. When an FBI agent in

Phoenix, Ariz. noticed two months before the attacks that Middle Eastern men were taking flying lessons in his backyard and alerted headquarters that something ghastly might be in the offing, agents in Washington took no action. And a month later, when a group of agents in Minnesota warned that a French-born Moroccan named Zacarias Moussaoui was in the area illegally and trying to learn how to fly a commercial jet, officials at FBI headquarters never put the two warnings together. In the culture of the FBI, agents were not champions at imagining crimes that had not been committed; they were simply supposed to investigate crimes after they occurred.

> *The FBI has begun to try to change its narrow way of thinking.*

The FBI has begun to try to change its narrow way of thinking. Today disrupting a terrorist group gets top priority, and if secrecy is lost, blowing the chances of a successful prosecution, so be it. Director Robert Mueller has replaced nearly all the bureau's mid-level executives, and many of the agents who were over 50 have retired. Agents are being told they can no longer simply construct an edifice of known facts, as they would for a traditional prosecution. They must instead look around corners and try to understand a terrorist's intentions, habits, methods and psychology. And where the agency once turned tips around with the speed of a turtle, it now operates on a hair trigger, often disseminating information about potential suspects and plots before it has been corroborated by multiple sources. Even the wispiest bits of data are quickly fed to the entire intelligence community and in many cases to 18,000 local and state police agencies. "That's a sea change," says a top FBI executive, who adds a comment the rest of the world discovered a decade ago: "The power of information is in letting it go."

Fixing the Hardware Problem: Before 9/11, many FBI offices had ancient green-screen computers with no Internet access. Like scriveners from another century, agents wrote their reports out in longhand and often in triplicate. In fact, until a few months ago, many agents were still communicating with one another—and with outsiders—via fax. Some agents kept their best information in shoe boxes under their desks because they didn't trust the computer security system. That's hardly surprising after it turned out that one of their own—FBI security and computer whiz Robert Hanssen—had been working for the Soviets and the Russians for more than a decade. In the years leading up to the attack, noted one of the bureau's top computer analysts, the FBI has "lacked effective data-mining capabilities and analytical tools. It has often been unable to retrieve key information and analyze it in a timely manner, and a lot has probably slipped through the cracks as a result."

In the past two years, Mueller has accelerated a long-overdue computer overhaul called Trilogy, which he says promises "worldwide high-speed data communications networks . . . to share all kinds of data, to include video and images, among all of our FBI offices throughout the world." Now all field personnel have late-model desktop computers. It will still take months to replace the computers at the bureau's massive Pennsylvania Avenue headquarters. And it is only this year that many FBI agents have finally got e-mail.

> *Ever since 9/11, the fight over turf has been peaceful compared with the fight over money.*

Making the System Accountable: One of the biggest weaknesses exposed by 9/11 was the lack of a single, integrated government clearinghouse for terrorist threats. A single center would ensure that information would be spread around liberally and that someone could ultimately be held accountable. But instead of just one clearinghouse, there are more threat centers than ever before. Each agency—the CIA, the FBI and the Department of Homeland Security—has its own analytical or operations center, and some have both. Several agencies still produce separate watch lists of terrorists operating worldwide. Last week Congress grew impatient with what seemed to be an exploding universe of terrorist information and action centers in Washington. "Right now there is more confusion than clarity," said an exasperated Representative Jim Turner of Texas, speaking at a hearing Tuesday afternoon. "Surely, almost two years after Sept. 11 of 2001, we could come up with one consistent watch list."

And accountability, never a Washington strong suit, remains elusive. It was during the State of the Union address in January that Bush asked for the creation of a single independent center to coordinate all terrorist threats. The center finally opened a few months ago, after weeks of predictable bureaucratic warfare. Housed temporarily at the CIA, it is known around Washington as the TTIC— or TeeTick—for Terrorist Threat Integration Center. Home to 100 agents, analysts and computer whizzes from half a dozen agencies, the TTIC is supposed to be the four-chambered heart through which information passes from original source to all arms and legs of the governments—state, local and federal.

But who is responsible if, as Connecticut Republican Chris Shays asked at a House hearing last week, "some bit of intelligence is not properly viewed or vetted for what it is and something bad happens as a result? Who takes responsibility?" He didn't really get an answer. Why? Said a witness: "It's not clear on the bureaucratic chart where this lands."

Following the Money: Ever since 9/11, the fight over turf has been peaceful compared with the fight over money. While people often think the CIA director controls a vast intelligence empire, his realm pales in comparison with that of the Secretary of Defense. The CIA administers only about 15% to 20% of the annual intelligence budget. The rest is in the hands of the Pentagon, which has long had the final say over where the satellites go to spy and where the eavesdropping ships drop anchor and listen. But just when it makes sense to give the CIA director more power to track the kind of enemy that conventional armies and navies are not trained to detect or fight, the agency often lacks the clout to do so.

In the past several years, a growing chorus of intelligence experts, led by former National Security Adviser Brent Scowcroft, has called on Congress and the White House to place all the budget authority in the hands of a single Cabinet-level intelligence chief. But the Bush Administration has ignored these calls, partly because Pentagon chief Donald Rumsfeld has no intention of giving away power without a fight and partly because the White House has no desire to pick a fight with him. It was therefore striking that the Pentagon came under such heavy fire in last week's bipartisan report for resisting requests made by CIA Director Tenet before 9/11, when the agency wanted to use satellites and other military hardware to spot and target terrorists in Afghanistan.

Facing the Saudi Problem: Perhaps the biggest unsolved mystery left over from the attacks is, How much help—financial and otherwise—does bin Laden get from old friends in Saudi Arabia, and why hasn't the U.S. dealt more harshly with the Saudi problem? Treasury officials have been arguing for months to come down harder on Saudis who were giving cash to known bin Laden charity fronts. Last year Princess Haifa al-Faisal, wife of the Saudi ambassador to the U.S., Prince Bandar bin Sultan, was found to have given money directly to the family of a Saudi man in San Diego who befriended and assisted two of the 9/11 hijackers. Yet the Administration acted as if she had merely misplaced her ATM card. Some branches of the Saudi royal family (a clan with 7,000 princes) actively cultivate ties with radical groups to gain political support in their own country, according to a former senior White House aide. Yet in Washington mere mention of a Riyadh connection with the war on terrorism remains a weird taboo. The Administration forced the joint panel to black out 28 straight pages of testimony about Saudi financial support for terrorists.

In their defense, U.S. officials say they are much harsher with the oil-rich royal family in private than they would ever be in public. And they add that Riyadh is finally beginning, after years of denial, to realize that it must pull its head out of the sand and actively join the war on terrorism. The May 12 bombings of two Western enclaves in Riyadh have moved the Saudi government to take the threat seriously. "Things were progressing on the counterterrorism front with the Saudis before May 12," said the former Bush aide, "and things have continued to get better since then." The former aide argues that the U.S. has an interest in maintaining that momentum and that the White House gains additional leverage with Riyadh by protecting it.

The authors of the 900-page report issued last week made many other recommendations for the ongoing war on terrorism. They cited a need for more Arabic speakers, deeper penetration of terrorist cells by U.S. agents and stronger cooperation with foreign intelligence agencies—as well as more money for just about everything. And the lawmakers also called on the government to keep the public better informed about the complex dangers and difficult choices we now face than it did in the days and weeks before 9/11.

Nothing to quarrel with there. But in the war on terrorism, there are always going to be two fronts: one with a shadowy enemy who is constantly trying to exploit our weaknesses, and another with ourselves. In that battle, we face complacency, bureaucracy and our own reluctance to change. Like the war on terrorism itself, this battle requires constant vigilance.

Mission Impossible?[2]

By Jean Kumagai
IEEE Spectrum, April 2003

What the FBI doesn't know can kill you. That, at least, is what we've been led to believe since 9/11.

Had agents in Minnesota been allowed to search Zacarias Moussaoui's computer, had the Phoenix office memo warning of Al Qaeda members enrolling at U.S. aviation schools filtered up the chain of command, had the internal computer databases done anything but the most rudimentary searches, maybe, just maybe, things might have gone much differently 18 months ago. But for the failure to connect those proverbial dots, 3000 lives might have been saved.

The idea that 9/11 could have been prevented heightens the tragedy, of course, but also invites all kinds of speculation: if we accept the premise, then there must exist some deliberate course of action that we should now take. Experts and officials have spent the last year and a half trying to figure out what that course should be, but have reached no clear agreement.

Understandably, much attention has focused on the Federal Bureau of Investigation (FBI), both for what it could have done but didn't, and for what it should do now. The post-9/11 revelations of mistakes and mismanagement only underscored what many had said for years: that the bureau's fundamental organizational, cultural, and technological deficiencies have bred a swarm of high-profile gaffes [see "FBI Under Fire," pp. 76–77] and render it unsuited to the intricacies of fighting terrorism.

As for improving, under Robert S. Mueller III, sworn in as director a week before the September 2001 attacks, the bureau has announced a broad agenda of technological initiatives and long-sought organizational reforms. Some of that is merely catch-up, like upgrading the FBI's antiquated computational infrastructure to an acceptable, but by no means advanced, standard. More exploratory efforts, though, in investigative data warehousing and information-sharing networks, could, if successful, place the agency for a change on the technological cutting edge. As the nation's leading agency for domestic terrorism and federal law enforcement, Mueller has said, the FBI "should be the most technologically proficient investigative agency in the world."

First, though, he'll have to bring the bureau into the 21st century, technically as well as culturally, and beef up its capabilities in intelligence gathering and analysis. Then he'll have to fend off a growing chorus of critics intent on divesting the bureau of its domestic intelligence responsibilities. Also to be addressed are the concerns of privacy and civil liberties advocates. With the FBI's powers greatly expanded under the USA PATRIOT Act, they fear the innovations being put into place are just the first steps in setting up a police state.

Lastly, there are the many unresolved technical questions: is it really possible to build a system that can precisely identify a crime's precursors, when the would-be perpetrators are doing their utmost to be untraceable and unpredictable? And is the FBI the right outfit to build such a system?

"It's the Leadership"

In September, a blue-ribbon panel of business leaders, lawyers, and academics known as the Markle Foundation Task Force on National Security concluded that "among other things, [the FBI] has failed to develop an adequate strategic plan, has no comprehensive strategic human capital plan, has personnel with inadequate language skills, antiquated computer hardware and

---

Nobody should have been surprised by the sorry state of the FBI's computers. The problems date back at least 10 years.

---

software, no enterprise architecture, and several disabling cultural traditions." Three months later, the Department of Justice's inspector general weighed in with a scathing report about the FBI's mismanagement of its information technology (IT) programs: "The FBI continues to spend hundreds of millions of dollars on IT projects without adequate assurance that these projects will meet their intended goals."

For all the finger-pointing, though, nobody should have been surprised by the sorry state of the FBI's computers. The problems date back at least 10 years. "I wrote a book in 1993 about the FBI and even then I was critical about their computer systems, the fact that they had to double up on computers, and the systems were very backward," says Ronald Kessler, author of *The Bureau: The Secret History of the FBI* (St. Martin's Press, 2002). "Some people say, 'FBI agents don't like computers,' but that's not true. They all use computers at home that in many cases are better than what they have at work. It's not the agents, it's the leadership."

Kessler is optimistic about Mueller, an ex-Marine and former federal prosecutor who is reputed to be reform minded and tech friendly. He is said to carry a PDA, use e-mail, and make Power-Point presentations from his laptop—activities his predecessor, Louis Freeh, seldom if ever engaged in. After becoming the U.S. attorney for San Francisco, Mueller led an overhaul of the office's computer system for tracking cases; the new program, called Alcatraz, is now used by all U.S. attorneys. Upon arriving at the FBI, Mueller asked that Microsoft Office be installed on his desktop. "They told him, 'We can put it on there, but it won't be compatible with anything else in the FBI,'" says Kessler. "He hit the roof."

The fall of 2001 saw the start of an ambitious program of modernization, which seems to recognize that the barriers that prevent the FBI from analyzing and sharing data are as much cultural as technological. As outlined by Mueller and other agency leaders in regular appearances before Congress, these include:

- Accelerating a bureau-wide overhaul of basic computer hardware, software, and network infrastructure. The three-year, US $534 million effort known as Trilogy will eventually give each of the 11,400 FBI agents and 16,400 other employees a Dell Pentium desktop PC running Microsoft Office, with secure, high-speed connections to FBI headquarters and hundreds of field and satellite offices. In early March, Mueller announced that the first phase of this upgrade had been completed.

- Replacing the FBI's ancient DOS-based Automated Case Support (ACS) database with a more user-friendly Windows-based system that can search on not just text but also photos, video, and audio records. Known as the Virtual Case File system, it's set to come online by the end of 2003.

- Creating Web versions of the bureau's most commonly used investigative tools for accessing, organizing, and analyzing data.

- Hiring 350 intelligence analysts and 900 special agents, with special emphasis on those trained in the physical sciences, computer science, and engineering, as well as foreign languages, military intelligence, and counterterrorism.

FBI Under Fire

27 July 1996
Pipe bomb explodes at Atlanta Olympics; three days later FBI arrests security guard Richard Jewell. Cleared of all charges three months later, Jewell issues a statement: "In its rush to show the world how quickly it could get its man, the FBI trampled on my rights as a citizen....[The] FBI and the media almost destroyed me and my mother."

June 2000
ISI is revamped and renamed eFBI; after initial objections, Congress agrees to fund it.

18 February 2001
FBI agent Robert Hanssen is arrested for spying for Soviets and Russians over a 22-year period.

10 July 2001
So-called Phoenix Memo is sent by FBI agent Ken Williams to FBI counterterrorism division, suggesting Middle Eastern students at an Arizona flight school could be Al Qaeda agents training for hijackings.

13 September 2000
Los Alamos scientist Wen Ho Lee, accused of selling nuclear secrets to China, is freed after nine months in solitary confinement. A Justice Department report later faults the FBI for seriously mishandling the four-year investigation.

May–June 2001
FBI selects Dyncorp and SAIC as lead contractors for eFBI, now known as Trilogy.

March 1998
FBI proposes three-year, US $430 million Information Sharing Initiative (ISI) to provide the bureau with "a comprehensive computing infrastructure." Congress rejects request out of concern over implementation and management of past IT projects.

10 May 2001
Execution of Oklahoma City bomber Timothy McVeigh is postponed for a month after Justice Department reveals the FBI failed to provide his defense lawyers with more than 3000 documents.

1990   2000   2001

- Initiating a pilot study for an information-sharing network among field offices located in St. Louis; San Diego, Calif.; Seattle, Wash.; Portland, Ore.; Norfolk, Va.; and Baltimore. If successful, it could link all field offices and other agencies, too.

- Creating a corps of reports officers (long part of the Central Intelligence Agency and other agencies) responsible for identifying and collecting intelligence from FBI investigations and sharing that information with the intelligence community.

A Billion Records and Counting

Of the many announced reforms, probably the most provocative is the FBI's plan to engage in investigative data mining and data warehousing, with a view to detecting and connecting the traces of terrorist and criminal activity. Details are still sketchy, but presumably it would copy the techniques the commercial sector uses to track and predict consumer behavior, prevent IT network break-ins, and so on. (Repeated requests for interviews for this article were declined or went unanswered by bureau press officers; FBI contractors referred all questions to the bureau.)

"Data warehousing involves connecting various datasets from various sources—transactional data from your Web site, demographics data from providers like Axciom and Experian—and then using analytical software to detect patterns in the data, so that you can personalize the services you offer or detect fraud," explains data mining expert Jesus Mena.

There are two basic approaches, he says. "In the first, you look for outliers or deviations, things that are way outside normal behavior—somebody trying to access a computer network in the middle of the night, for example. The other is where you have a pattern of known activity and you have a signature that you try to match."

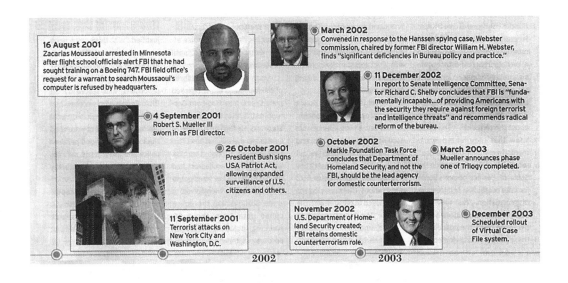

16 August 2001
Zacarias Moussaoui arrested in Minnesota after flight school officials alert FBI that he had sought training on a Boeing 747. FBI field office's request for a warrant to search Moussaoui's computer is refused by headquarters.

March 2002
Convened in response to the Hanssen spying case, Webster commission, chaired by former FBI director William H. Webster, finds "significant deficiencies in Bureau policy and practice."

11 December 2002
In report to Senate Intelligence Committee, Senator Richard C. Shelby concludes that FBI is "fundamentally incapable...of providing Americans with the security they require against foreign terrorist and intelligence threats" and recommends radical reform of the bureau.

4 September 2001
Robert S. Mueller III sworn in as FBI director.

26 October 2001
President Bush signs USA Patriot Act, allowing expanded surveillance of U.S. citizens and others.

October 2002
Markle Foundation Task Force concludes that Department of Homeland Security, and not the FBI, should be the lead agency for domestic counterterrorism.

March 2003
Mueller announces phase one of Trilogy completed.

11 September 2001
Terrorist attacks on New York City and Washington, D.C.

November 2002
U.S. Department of Homeland Security created; FBI retains domestic counterterrorism role.

December 2003
Scheduled rollout of Virtual Case File system.

2002   2003

Mena's book *Investigative Data Mining for Security and Criminal Detection* (Digital Press, 2003) discusses how these commercially available techniques can be applied to law enforcement and intelligence. The FBI, he notes, has long been a customer of ChoicePoint (Atlanta, Ga.), which collects and sells consumer information. To detect criminal or terrorist behavior, he says, one would overlay that data with data from law enforcement (for example, arrest records, photographs, and fingerprints), immigration (visa records and border crossings), and intelligence (terrorist watchlists and the like).

At least in theory, this is exactly what the FBI needs in order to know what it knows. It has amassed criminal and intelligence-related data galore—over a billion records, by one bureau estimate, stored in many databases at dozens of sites. Only a fraction of the FBI's data is in a common format that can be easily searched, analyzed, and shared. The agency's $680 million Integrated Automated Fingerprint Identification System (IAFIS), for example, contains millions of digital fingerprint records and has cut search time from weeks to hours. But it is not directly linked to the FBI's main network for handling case files, which is a text-only system. What's more, many state and local agencies still lack the equipment to access the IAFIS and upload and download prints. Nor, needless to say, is there a universal interface for allowing the databases at all the agencies to talk to one another, although some data exchanging—between, for example, the FBI and the U.S. Immigration and Naturalization Service (now the Bureau of Citizenship and Immigration Services)—has begun since 9/11.

Reportedly, the bureau now maintains a production line of scanners and optical character recognition software to convert some 750,000 paper documents a day into electronic text. Key files relating to counterterrorism going back 10 years, some 40 million or so pages, have already been converted. Still, at the current rate, it will take more than three and one-half years to convert the rest. And more paper is being generated all the time.

Take the FBI's handling of last fall's sniper attacks in and around Washington, D.C. As described by William Hooton, assistant director of the FBI's records management division, in a 14 November speech to the Association for Information and Image Management (Washington, D.C.), the bureau set up a phone center to field tips from the general public. Staff members duly logged each call on paper forms, which were collected every hour and taken to FBI headquarters, where they were scanned and the digital images fed into a bureau-wide database.

All the same, as an article in *Federal Computer Week* pointed out, a scanned handwritten note is not an electronically searchable file. That may explain why the bureau did not discover until after the fact that eyewitnesses had reported spotting the suspects' car, including its New Jersey license plates, at a handful of the crime scenes.

"They're seen at one crime scene and then they're seen again at another one miles away. That's an incident in itself—why were they there?" observes Mena. "That's clearly a failure to connect the dots, to see a recurring pattern of sightings of a car with out-of-state plates."

So-called free forms, of the kind used in the sniper attacks, present an enormous obstacle for data analysis, Mena says. "Someone might describe an individual as being tan or having an accent or dressed a certain way, and different investigators will enter that information differently." The solution, he says, is "to standardize from the beginning, so that you use checklists, as opposed to free forms, to capture the data." Text-mining software from companies like Autonomy, HNC, and IBM could then be used to categorize and organize the raw data automatically.

The FBI has not revealed whether or to what extent it has implemented such techniques. Last September, though, Mark Tanner, the FBI's information resources manager, told *Government Executive* magazine that he receives "probably 10 to 15 calls or e-mails a

---

All the data mining in the world will never trace the hand-written, hand-delivered messages that Osama bin Laden's Al Qaeda operatives allegedly use.

---

day from [vendors] who have solutions to these problems," but "we're unable to really implement them . . . because we don't have the infrastructure."

Standards matter all the more when information must be shared across agencies. The Department of Justice, which oversees the FBI, actually has a standards registry for just that purpose (see *http://it.ojp.gov/jsr/public/list.jsp*). It covers everything from message sets (IEEE 1512) to "the Interchange of Fingerprint, Facial, Scar Mark and Tattoo (SMT) Information." XML, the Extensible Markup Language, is one of the most widely discussed, in the FBI and elsewhere; there's now an XML standard for rap sheets and criminal histories. Taking that one step further, a group called the Organization for the Advancement of Structured Information Standards formed a technical committee in January to develop an XML framework for sharing criminal and terrorist evidence.

Filtering data in hopes of detecting a criminal or terrorist plot is not easy, Mena cautions. [The German federal police's recent exercise in data mining proved this to be true.] Unlike consumers, terrorists are not prone to repetition. "So you have to anticipate new types of attacks—bombings, or bioterrorism, or other activities," he says. And all the data mining in the world will never trace the hand-written, hand-delivered messages that Osama bin Laden's Al

Qaeda operatives allegedly use. "That's why a combination of human knowledge and machine learning is the best approach," Mena says.

Privacy and civil liberties advocates have a larger concern. "The FBI will now be conducting fishing expeditions using the services of the people who decide what catalogs to send you or what spam e-mail you will be interested in," says James Dempsey, executive director of the Center for Democracy and Technology (Washington, D.C.). "The problem is, the direct marketers can only call you during dinner time or mail you another credit card offer based on that information—the FBI can arrest you."

"We don't want to arrive at a situation where individuals are reluctant to, let's say, purchase a copy of the Koran from Amazon.com," agrees Steven Aftergood, a senior research analyst at the Federation of American Scientists (Washington, D.C.). "That would be intolerable." There need to be realistic error-correcting procedures, which in many cases do not now exist, not just for statistical or data-processing errors, but also for those introduced by "willful, deliberate abuse," he says. "The error-correction process should not be a knock on the door from the FBI."

Even with perfect data, data mining may yield a completely inaccurate picture. "It is all too easy to do Monday-morning quarterbacking and say 'Why didn't you connect the dots to see that stick of dynamite?' when in fact the same dots could be connected just as well to show a duck or a coffee mug," one computer expert with extensive training in intelligence work told *IEEE Spectrum*. Skeptical of both the technical capabilities and the political ramifications of the FBI's expanded surveillance efforts, he believes the technology will be "totally ineffective in its professed purpose [of catching terrorists] but too effective as a domestic police state tool."

Tyranny of the Case File

Of the many wrenching revelations to emerge after 9/11, none resonated quite like the report that the FBI's antiquated computer database could perform only single-word searches, on "flight" or "school," say, but not "flight school."

The story confirmed everyone's worst fears about the FBI's out-of-date abilities. Too bad it wasn't true. "It's bullshit," says Nancy Savage, a 26-year FBI veteran based in Portland, Ore. "I just go crazy reading what I read in the press, it's absolutely wrong."

The database in question is a DOS-based system that runs on the FBI's own secure network, says Savage, who is also president of the FBI Agents Association. Known as the Automated Case Support (ACS) system, it's used by thousands of agents each day. "I can search on 'flight schools' and do Boolean searches, I can pull up the full text of any document that's created in-house," Savage says.

The ACS also shows links to records at other agencies, local, state, and federal. "I can see that Seattle has something in their files that was created in the U.S. attorney's office on this date," Savage explains. "If I need it, then I can call or e-mail them, and they'll send it—it's pretty easy." (The notorious FBI spy Robert Hanssen was said to be a devoted ACS user, accessing not only classified records that he then sold to the Russians, but also searching on his own name and address and terms like DEAD DROP AND KGB to see if any records pointed to him.)

That said, the ACS has a multitude of problems and is slated for replacement under the Trilogy computer upgrade. Although unveiled in 1995, it's 1980s-era technology: mainframe-based, user-unfriendly, text-only. Because it is three applications cobbled together, each with its own set of commands, a simple search can mean delving down through several DOS screens and remembering at each step which function key (no pointing and clicking here) corresponds to which command.

The ACS's fatal flaw, though, is that it simply automated already onerous administrative chores. Over the course of its 95-year history, the FBI's bureaucracy has devised some 900 standard forms, to be filled out for everything from recording attendance (Form 420) to filing a memorandum (Form 467) to conducting an interview (Form 302). Until very recently, the FBI's automation approach was "to just build macros for everything," says Savage. "If I'm working on a fugitive case, I've got to remember these seven macros I have to go through. You become a huge bureaucrat, doing one hour of investigation and seven hours of administration."

The Virtual Case File system looks to be better, she notes. "You can't just automate, you have to reengineer," she says. This time around, experienced street agents are being brought into the development process. "Every form is being examined. Can we get rid of it? Can we do this automatically? It should make us incredibly more productive." Data input into the system is being streamlined, and the extra bandwidth being added through the Trilogy upgrade will allow photos and video to be uploaded and downloaded. Querying the system will yield, among much else, a linked diagram of where each relevant document resides.

Still unanswered is whether the new system could help move the FBI beyond the "tyranny of the case file," as Senator Richard Shelby (R-Ala.) terms it. In a harsh assessment of the U.S. intelligence community released in December, Shelby noted that "fundamentally, the FBI is a law enforcement organization." Investigating crimes, though, is quite different from gathering and analyzing intelligence data in hopes of preventing terrorism. Bureau agents are trained to view information in terms of building a case—"a discrete bundle of information the fundamental purpose of which is to prove elements of crimes against specific potential defendants in a court of law." An agent's success is measured largely by how many arrests, prosecutions, and convictions he or she achieves.

Intelligence analysts, by contrast, have little concern about the data's admissibility in court, tending "to reach conclusions based upon disparate fragments of data derived from widely distributed sources and assembled into a probabilistic 'mosaic' of information." A good intelligence worker is not looking to arrest a suspect; that would only serve to cut off vital information about the suspect's plans and contacts and perhaps even the opportunity to recruit the suspect as a double agent.

Shelby is among those unconvinced that the FBI can reform sufficiently to become an effective intelligence agency. Among the options outlined in his report are: placing the bureau's counterintelligence and counterterrorism programs into a stand-alone agency; creating a semi-autonomous organization that would still report to the FBI but would in every other respect be separate from its law enforcement activities; and moving domestic intelligence to the Department of Homeland Security.

"Whatever the best answer turns out to be," Shelby concluded, "I believe some kind of radical reform of the FBI is in order—indeed, is long overdue."

To Probe Further

Recent critiques of the FBI's IT and intelligence capabilities include the U.S. Department of Justice Inspector General's *Federal Bureau of Investigation's Information Technology Investments*, available online at *http://www.usdoj.gov/oig/audit/0309/0309.pdf*, and Senator Richard Shelby's *September 11 and the Imperative of Reform in the U.S. Intelligence Community*, to be found at *http://intelligence.senate.gov/shelby.pdf*.

Digging Through Data for Omens[3]

By Dana Hawkins
U.S. News & World Report, April 7, 2003

Annoyed at having to remove your shoes at airport security? Just wait. This month, the Transportation Security Administration began testing a screening program on some Delta Air Lines flights that would subject passengers to a whole new level of scrutiny. Here's the plan: Book a seat, and a computer data-sifting process matches your name, address, birth date, and ticket-purchasing information against financial and commercial databases and government watch lists. The goal is to verify your identity and look for any hint of a security risk. "Our system today is not as precise as it ought to be," says TSA spokesman Robert Johnson. "We don't want to waste more time focusing on grandmas."

If government officials have their way, the TSA's test is just the beginning of a new approach to security called data mining. Next year, the TSA's system will be fully in place, coding all travelers by color: green if they trip no alarms, yellow for further screening, or red if the system flags them as too dangerous to allow on board. Other agencies could deploy far more powerful technologies that would screen us all, to pinpoint among hundreds of millions of innocents anyone planning acts of terrorism. The technology would comb the vast amount of information—purchase records, E-mail and phone logs, travel arrangements—that people generate in their daily lives, looking for telltale patterns such as a purchase of fertilizer, a rented truck, and a series of trips to the Middle East.

The quest has had a rocky start. The Department of Defense's Total Information Awareness (TIA) program, a five-year effort, has committed $260 million so far to develop tools for large-scale data mining. But it ran into a public-relations fiasco after Vice Adm. John Poindexter of Iran-contra fame was named to lead the project. Its Orwellian name and a logo (since dropped) showing an all-seeing eye atop a pyramid didn't help. Congress recently voted to require the Pentagon to justify the program and seek approval before monitoring citizens. Yet politics and privacy fears have not halted the quest: TIA research is going strong, and smaller operations like TSA's are getting underway. The true stumbling block may be technology.

It's a delicate dual challenge: accurately spotting suspicious patterns across multiple databases while minimizing false alarms and safeguarding individual privacy. "It's a project similar in scale to

---

putting a man on the moon," says Usama Fayyad, a data-mining specialist who is CEO of digiMine. "It's going to take a national commitment, the best brains in the country, and many years to do it right."

Scientists were among the first to apply mathematical pattern-finding tools to databases—Fayyad led a data-mining project to identify distant celestial objects called quasars amid billions of ordinary stars and galaxies. Companies also mine data on consumers, analyzing buying habits to spot potential customers and monitoring credit card or phone use to detect fraud. Computers watch, for example, for a known credit card fraud pattern: a small gasoline purchase (to see if a card is valid) followed by a much bigger charge. Or they look for a common factor in events that seem unrelated—say, a series of insurance claims in the same ZIP code.

All-knowing

TIA would apply these strategies on a grander scale. Opponents initially feared it would develop a single centralized uber-database that would contain just about every imaginable scrap of information on all citizens. In fact, say officials, the database could be a virtual one, created by linking records already gathered by companies and the government. The government routinely draws on data collected by other groups, after all. The FBI buys personal data from aggregators like ChoicePoint, which compiles information from credit reports and public records. ChoicePoint is now expected to team up with Regulatory DataCorp, which draws on more than 20,000 sources, from news reports to criminal fugitive lists, to screen passengers for the TSA.

Data mining alarms civil libertarians, who are already attacking the TSA's screening program as a "government blacklist." Homeland security experts, for their part, say it would be folly to hobble such efforts. "We're throwing out our single greatest advantage over our foes, our technological expertise," says Paul Rosenzweig of the Heritage Foundation, a conservative think tank.

But both sides may be losing sight of the enormous practical difficulties: the sheer volume of data to be searched and the ability of savvy terrorists to change their modus operandi to avoid detection. Says Robert Grossman of the National Center for Data Mining at the University of Illinois–Chicago: "People aren't willing to accept that we'll miss some terrorist who may blow up a plane or that we'll hurt good people" by falsely identifying them as threats.

Such mistakes are inevitable. A new study by the Consumer Federation of America and the National Credit Reporting Association found that 10 percent of credit reports contain errors in names or other identifying information—yet such reports are one of the tools the TSA will use to verify identity. TIA researchers are looking for ways to cope with database errors, and they are also seeking "privacy-enhancing technologies" that, for example, would keep data anonymous until the system uncovered a suspicious pattern.

But even if those efforts succeed, there's the fear that the terrorist detection system itself could come under attack. Barbara Simons of the Association for Computing Machinery asks: "Is it even possible to put together a database with sensitive financial, medical, educational, communication, and travel records—without providing a new target for exploitation and attack by hackers and terrorists?" The country may soon find out.

Can We Be Safe *and* Free?[4]

By Gene Stephens
USA Today Magazine, January 2003

How much freedom are Americans willing to give up in exchange for safety from terrorists? Street criminals? Other lawbreakers? At what point does the loss of privacy and freedom of speech and movement outweigh the perception of added security? Can we have it all—civil liberties and safety?

Public policy is always about trade-offs and compromise. In this case, we cannot truly be free unless we have a reasonable degree of safety, but we cannot truly feel safe unless we are also secure from undue prying into our personal lives. Adding to our real or perceived sense of safety comes at the cost of watching us more closely to protect us from harm.

What Americans need is a comfortable balance between safety and freedom—belief we can say and do whatever and go wherever we want within the limits of the law without repercussions from criminals and terrorists and without repressive restrictions and surveillance by authorities—a difficult task. Having our cake and eating it too requires a precarious balancing act between high-tech and high-touch—development and use of some "gee whiz" gadgetry only to the point we feel relatively safe without feeling abused by the process. Airports already have become testing grounds for this post–Sept. 11 approach. Passengers want safety, but with a minimum of hassle; airlines want passengers at a cost low enough to make a profit; and regulators want to be seen as protecting the public without creating a bureaucratic nightmare.

A major test will occur as the million-dollar-plus "Total Recall"–type X-ray machines are pressed into general service in airports across the nation and later at public gathering places (stadiums, coliseums, fairgrounds) and government complexes (courthouses, administrative buildings, post offices). While these devices can spot any weapons or contraband (from razor blades to plastic bags of cocaine) right down to the bone, they also show the size and shape of body parts for security personnel and possibly others to see and evaluate. Snickers and derisive remarks likely will not be appreciated. When the handheld versions (already in testing) are issued to police at the street level, any and all citizens will be subject to search with these camcorder-size scanners. Absent any recourse to stop (or even know about) such searches, will modesty compel peo-

---

ple to wear lead underwear (and will that even divert the electronic device?) or provide a niche market for new "blocking" technology?

The war on terrorism has indeed provided a bonanza for tech developers and suppliers as well as public and private security providers. Federal laboratories have accelerated the pace of research and are turning out new products like the Sandia Decon Foam, which can be used in foam or gas versions to decontaminate many chemical and biological weapons, such as saran and anthrax. The National Institutes of Health, meanwhile, has developed biochips that are programmed to recognize various forms of bacteria and sound the alarm, with the DNA structures of new biological warfare agents being added to the memory as they appear. The military has turned to PackBot technology and has utilized a $40,000 prototype called Fester for radio-controlled reconnaissance in searching the caves of Afghanistan for Al Qaeda. (Fester was employed successfully in searching the debris in the World Trade Center for victims.) Also being used are the Predator, a low-flying

---

> *The war on terrorism has indeed provided a bonanza for tech developers and suppliers as well as public and private security providers.*

---

drone that fires antitank missiles, and the Global Hawk, an unmanned Air Force surveillance plane that tracks the enemy from 60,000 feet.

To thwart cyber attacks, biometric identification systems—from fingerprints and voice verification to keystroke and DNA analysis—are being perfected so everyone who logs onto the Internet can be identified immediately, ending anonymous surfing in cyberspace. This will become critical as cyber money replaces cash and credit/debit cards in the international economy of the future. This immediate ID on the Net will provide still more stored information on every user—eventually nearly all Americans and almost everyone on Earth.

Other intrusive technology includes facial recognition, universal DNA banks, ubiquitous cameras and computing, and neuromanipulation—all designed to find, observe, and capture a terrorist/criminal. Many communities are installing cameras in public places—often with federal funding—and soon may go to quasipublic and even private places in the name of public safety. In Los Angeles, motion-sensitive cameras in high-crime areas snap a picture when triggered and play a recorded warning: "We will use this photograph to prosecute you. Leave now." In Wilmington, Del., "jump out" squads of police descend on known drug areas and round up suspected dealers and interrogate them (for up to two hours), and take digital pictures of all others on the street to compile a suspect file. Add facial recognition scanning—as done in Tampa, Fla., and Virginia Beach, Va.—to this, and almost anyone caught on camera can be identified. In England, where facial recognition and ubiquitous cameras have been used for some time, the public has seemingly accepted the loss of privacy, but expressed concern after learning that some public safety officers have been scanning videos of citizens in search of compromising positions (scratching, picking, adjusting, etc.), which they then show for fun and profit.

Creating universal DNA bar codes at birth will add to the ability to track everyone, especially when linked to computers where every word spoken or written is recorded and kept on file. In addition, there are reading of brainwaves and chemical manipulation of the brain to alter attitudes and behavior. The chemical cocktails being developed by neuroscientists challenge a basic belief of most Americans and a cornerstone of U.S. law—that individuals act of their own free will and are thus responsible for their behavior. Increasingly, these brain researchers have discovered that emotions and thinking processes can be explained by chemical makeup of the brain and that changes in that makeup will alter the individual's behavior—deterrence and/or rehabilitation by injection!

> *Some applaud the arrival of this "Brave New World" where crime . . . is likely to be observed, recorded, punished, and deterred.*

Some applaud the arrival of this "Brave New World" where crime (and any other aberrant behavior) is likely to be observed, recorded, punished, and deterred. Leaders of the Communitarian movement see it simply as a needed switch from individual to community rights—necessary crime prevention. After all, authorities are often fond of saying, "If you're not doing anything wrong, you have nothing to fear."

As the Homeland Security budget escalates, money will be available for even-more-innovative, effective surveillance and detection equipment and systems, as well as "first strike defense" mechanisms—such as more-efficient smart bombs and missiles, faster and more-mobile military units, and specialized terrorism squads in law enforcement agencies. The technology discussed above and the additional innovations below are either available now or in the development and/or testing stage and can be expected to be in use by the end of this decade.

In law enforcement agencies, ubiquitous devices will be monitored in high-tech surveillance complexes that provide instant video and auditory access to anyone in the jurisdiction. (In Rio de Janeiro, Brazil, a police blimp uses cameras to watch about 350 high-crime areas constantly.) Some officers will have bionic eyes and ears that see and hear through walls, making anything citizens do in their homes or offices "in plain view" of the police. Nanosized computer chips implanted in their brains (organic biochips) will allow many officers instantly to identify any citizen and access a birth-to-death dossier from universal DNA data banks to assess the likelihood of that individual committing a crime or other deviant act. The biochips could provide police with constant updates of all new technological advancements, such as forced memory recall through brain scanning with electrodes (e.g., of the night of the killing, the sexual misconduct incident, the illegal use of a computer) and memory transfer (e.g., from the suspect to a data bank for later use in investigation or as evidence). Brainwave lie detector scanners will be available for interrogation, along with universal language translators and devices to overpower psychological defenses attempted by the suspect.

In courts, visuals taken directly from the memory banks of the defendant, as well as of the accuser, will be available for evidence. Jurors can be chosen at random from a global venire and can view the trial from their home or office, where they will have access to all evidence and testimony worldwide. Virtual reality enactments of the incident and aftermath, including the trail of evidence leading to the defendant, will make the alleged crime and its perpetration seem real indeed (as demonstrated in 2001 in the "cyber court" at William & Mary School of Law). It will be possible to feed all the evidence into an artificially intelligent supercomputer (AI Judge) to determine probability of guilt and the appropriate penalty/reparations for the offense.

For many, community-based surveillance and control will be the correctional sentence, carried out via an electronic-electroshock body implant that uses the global positioning system (GPS) to track the convicted offender (and possibly an individual "predicted" to offend). The whereabouts of the probationer will be known at all times. As long as the approved schedule is followed (e.g., school, work, therapy, community service), nothing happens, but any deviation results in automatic, convulsive electroshock until the subject returns to the approved area and schedule. Biochip implants will be available for subliminal conditioning (e.g., "Do as you are told"; "Follow the rules") to control the current or potential future offender further. For those deemed too dangerous (e.g., violent, chronic, politically deviant) to be allowed to remain in society, possible alternatives include space prisons, where inmates mine asteroids to pay for their keep; undersea prisons, where they perform aquaculture (e.g., grow seaweed to feed the world's starving); or suspended animation, where vital fluids are removed and the individual is stored and then reanimated at time of release.

For drug addicts or persons found to be genetically prone to addiction, sober-up implants (now undergoing human testing) could extinguish the intoxicating effects of drugs—from alcohol to cocaine and heroin to designer compounds. Other nanoimplants could surge through the body in a constant search for biological abnormalities (e.g., a low serotonin level that could lead to agitated, aggressive behavior) and correct most dysfunctions (e.g., stimulate serotonin production) and warn authorities of potential problems. The ultimate prevention tool likely will be genetic reengineering—alter, insert, or delete a gene, and create a person incapable of committing criminal or terrorist acts. The next step might be to clone these crime-free individuals.

The high-tech scenario above, while well supported by current ongoing research and testing, has shocked, even repulsed, everyone from students to parents, politicians, and police when presented to them by this writer. Although many approve of some aspects of this approach, the overall scheme is rejected as simply unacceptable in a free society. Loss of privacy, "Gestapo tactics," and dehumanization are the three most-cited complaints. What privacy would anyone have in this ubiquitous surveillance community? Wouldn't the Nazi Gestapo have loved to have had this type of technology to control the populace? What is the role of the individual in this new "safe" society? Must it come down to a person being simply a carbon unit to be manipulated and rendered impotent for the "good" of the masses?

Have the terrorists succeeded beyond their expectations by setting the U.S. on a course of suppression of the rights Americans cherish most—freedom of speech, expression, and movement? How much

---

Wouldn't the Nazi Gestapo have loved to have had this type of technology to control the populace?

---

further should we go in the name of safety, and is this assault on the individual and civil liberties productive in providing real protection? Is it possible there are no technological solutions to crime and terrorism? After all, technology is amoral. It can be used to enslave or enhance humankind. Where society goes in the future will depend on how human institutions and their operatives use technology and cope with the issues and dilemmas posed by it.

New Directions

Real safety, as noted earlier, depends on being both physically safe from harm and able to exercise one's personal liberties. After 9/11, many Americans felt so unsafe physically they believed they had to give up some liberties—especially privacy and freedom of movement—in order to achieve a modicum of security. Almost half (49%) of respondents to a poll taken nearly a year after the terrorist attack said First Amendment rights go too far in protecting free speech and particularly freedom of religion. More significantly, perhaps, 41% said media criticism of military policy should be banned.

In a poll shortly after the event, a large majority expressed willingness to endure long waits and personal searches at airports and public gathering places, but the size of the majority began to dissipate as, despite the inconvenience, those testing the systems put in place found them easy to thwart—carrying knives, razors, cutting tools, and even handguns through security checks. A poll marking the one-year anniversary of the attack found Americans had come to terms with their new reality: 75% had little confidence the government could prevent future attacks and 60% thought such attacks were inevitable. Few felt capturing or killing Al Qaeda head Osama bin Laden (and only two percent believed he was already dead) and Iraqi dictator Saddam Hussein would stop future terrorism against the U.S., but 82% said they had not and would not let the terrorist acts change their lifestyles in any permanent or significant way.

The voices present just days after Sept. 11 are growing louder—suggesting that a high-tech war on terrorism and high-tech, repressive security are not the answers to the safety issue. Obscured by feelings of fear and anger, and a demand for retribution, have been what some say are more-effective and less-draconian measures.

Fear itself is a major stumbling block to security and, to a large extent, research indicates the pervasive fear in America today is simply not justified. Despite 9/11, there was no more terrorism (in

---

Fear itself is a major stumbling block to security.

---

fact, somewhat less) in the world in 2001 and 2002 than there was in 2000 and earlier years, and street crime in America is far below the levels of a decade ago. The FBI's Uniform Crime Reports show a constant drop from the early 1990s through 2000, with a slight increase in some categories in 2001, while the self-reporting system of the Bureau of Justice's National Crime Victimization Survey indicates major household crime (including rape and assault) in the U.S. dropped significantly from 1974 to the present.

In *Creating Fear: News and the Construction of Crisis*, popular culturalist David L. Altheide writes about the "discourse of fear"—"the awareness and expectation that danger and risk are lurking everywhere"—that news media and social control agencies have created in recent years, even before Sept. 11, but certainly accelerated by the terrorists' attack. Such fear serves the media to obtain reader-listener-viewership, while providing monetary, legal, and citizen support for law enforcement and other government agencies to "solve" the problem. Altheide says fear perseveres "despite clear evidence that most citizens are healthier, safer, and happier than ever before."

In this climate of fear, "hawks" often gain the upper hand by insisting disaster is ahead unless the "enemy" is exterminated and the military/enforcement strength is enhanced to deter future attacks/crimes. While most Americans have supported a military strike as one option, few feel this will provide safety or solve the problem. In this environment, Americans are likely to continue to endure some inconveniences and intrusions (i.e., questioning, surveillance, producing identification on demand) by officials, but with no real belief that this will make them significantly safer from terrorists, they are unlikely to give up any basic liberties permanently or even for a lengthy period of time.

The stage seems set then for a search for new directions in the fight against crime and terrorism. Maybe it's time for more high-touch initiatives. Possibly the best explanation for the sharp decrease in street crime in the U.S. over the last decade has been the "weed-and-seed" approach taken in most cities and many rural police agencies. Whereas technology can't be used in this strategy, the major thrust is to weed out current problems by using street-sweeping ordinances (e.g., vagrancy, loitering, public drunkenness, and drug possession) to get the immediate problem individuals off the streets and behind bars, even if for only a short time. Then the "seed" must be planted—everything from job training to schools with nurseries for teenage mothers to assistance in budgeting and housekeeping and after-school jobs and recreation programs for students—so the neighborhood will gain pride in its possibilities and refuse to put up with drug dealing, burglary, assault, and other crimes. Some of the best "seed" programs have involved tenant management of public housing, where residents have cleaned up their homes and grounds and demanded that anyone living there do the same and stay out of trouble with the law or face eviction. Combined with community-oriented policing, a partnership has evolved between police and citizens to do frequent needs analyses to determine what problems have the potential of creating crime-breeding situations and then jointly developing and carrying out a plan to solve them, often bringing public and private social services groups into the communal effort. Where this high-touch effort has been implemented fully, criminal activities have decreased.

> *The lasting residual of such programs is a more-aware community of citizens who have seen crime curtailed by their joint efforts with government agents.*

The lasting residual of such programs is a more-aware community of citizens who have seen crime curtailed by their joint efforts with government agents—residents who are less fearful and more confident that something can be done and their lives can be made safer by such partnerships. This may be what is needed to have any long-term impact on reducing the threat of terrorism.

After World War II, much of Europe and Asia was in ruins. President Harry Truman and other leaders of Allied countries instituted the Marshall Plan to rebuild the war-torn nations—including the Axis countries (e.g., Germany and Japan). Today, those nations are again socioeconomic powerhouses and can be counted as allies, rather than enemies. Maybe it's time for a similar 21st-century effort.

Despite the success of the Marshall Plan, the U.S. embarked on several additional conflicts (Korea, Vietnam) without much success, possibly because leaders lost sight of the road to peace—winning the "hearts and minds" of the people. In this ever-shrinking global village, the isolationism many Americans have craved is simply not possible. What happens in nations halfway around the world does affect life everywhere, including the U.S.

The circumstances that have led to terrorism by radical Muslims are complex and enduring. To some extent, military attacks on them simply strengthen their cause and draw sympathy to them from others. It also makes the most-powerful nation on Earth look like a bully—killing and destroying the property of poor people trying to eke out a living on less than $1 a day. This is no way to win hearts and minds. It is the way to lose friends and allies.

We are quite willing to "weed" out terrorists, but are we as willing and capable of providing the "seed" to alleviate the long-term dilemma? Can we help while respecting other nations' cultures, even when they are alien to our way of thinking? Can we become good neighbors in the international community, accepting our role as a partner, obligated by our position of wealth and power to share our resources and technology, and learning from others what they have to offer that can enrich our lives? The angry imperative, "Kill the infidels," resonates with many of the current multimillions of disenfranchised people in a world which is increasingly separated into haves and have-nots, with the divide growing ever wider. Providing assistance without patronizing can reduce the staggering numbers of world citizens in desperate need and mute the siren call of the religious fanatics. Only then, when all are safe—from hunger, homelessness, oppression, crime, and war (including attack from the U.S.)—can we truly be safe.

From A Guide to the PATRIOT Act[5]

BY DAHLIA LITHWICK AND JULIA TURNER
SLATE, SEPTEMBER 8–11, 2003

Part 1

What's hot for fall of 2003?

Well, the USA PATRIOT Act, for one thing. Although it passed in Congress almost without dissent in the aftermath of Sept. 11, it's suddenly being revisited, and this time around some of the folks holding opinions have actually *read the thing*. Among its detractors are 152 communities, including several major cities and three states, that have now passed resolutions denouncing the PATRIOT Act as an assault on civil liberties. More than one member of Congress has introduced legislation taking the teeth out of its most invasive provisions. And in a huge shock to the Justice Department, in July the so-called "Otter Amendment"—which de-funded the act's "sneak-and-peek" provision—passed in the House by a vote of 309-118. Introduced by a conservative Republican congressman from Idaho, C.L. "Butch" Otter, the amendment revealed the extent to which the PATRIOT Act engenders jitters across the political spectrum. Then there are the lawsuits, including one filed recently by the ACLU, urging the court to invalidate provisions of the act that threaten privacy or due process. All these reforms are wending their way through the system and the national consciousness as Americans start to take a sober second look at what the act really unleashed.

On the other hand, there's the John Ashcroft "PATRIOT Rocks" concert tour, launched last month, which has him visiting 18 cities and talking up the act to local law enforcement officials. The DOJ [Department of Justice] also unloosed a new Web site last month, designed to shore up support for the act. Ashcroft contends that had the PATRIOT Act been in place earlier, 9/11 wouldn't have happened and that absent a PATRIOT Act, the country may have seen more 9/11s over the past two years—a double-double negative that's unprovable, but enough to scare you witless. There have also been a raft of op-eds and articles—some evidently written by Ashcroft's U.S. attorneys at knifepoint—simultaneously making the point that the act has staved off unspeakable acts of terror while maintaining that it made only tiny infinitesimal changes to the existing laws.

Part of the impetus for all the new activity is that some of the really great bits of the act are set to sunset in 2005, and some Republican senators are planning to introduce legislation to repeal the sunset provisions altogether. Copies of "PATRIOT II"—the act that was intended to follow PATRIOT and grant the government even broader powers—were leaked to

How bad is PATRIOT, really? Hard to tell.

the press last winter, and while the ensuing ruckus ensured that PATRIOT II is dead, much of it will evidently rise again this fall in the guise of the VICTORY Act, Orrin Hatch's attempt to deploy PATRIOT powers in the war on drugs. One of the reasons that PATRIOT is fighting for its life, then, is so that its creepy progeny may someday live as well.

How bad is PATRIOT, really? Hard to tell. The ACLU, in a new fact sheet challenging the DOJ Web site, wants you to believe that the act threatens our most basic civil liberties. Ashcroft and his roadies call the changes in law "modest and incremental." Since almost nobody has read the legislation, much of what we think we know about it comes third-hand and spun. Both advocates and opponents are guilty of fear-mongering and distortion in some instances.

The truth of the matter seems to be that while some portions of the PATRIOT Act are truly radical, others are benign. Parts of the act formalize and regulate government conduct that was unregulated—and potentially even more terrifying—before. Other parts clearly expand government powers and allow it to spy on ordinary citizens in new ways. But what is most frightening about the act is exacerbated by the lack of government candor in describing its implementation. FOIA [Freedom of Information Act] requests have been half-answered, queries from the judiciary committee are blown off or classified. In the absence of any knowledge about how the act has been used, one isn't wrong to fear it in the abstract—to worry about its potential, since that is all we can know.

Ashcroft and his supporters on the stump cite a July 31 Fox News/Opinion Dynamics Poll showing that 91 percent of registered voters say the act had not affected their civil liberties. One follow-up question for them: How could they know?

If you haven't read all 300-plus pages of the legislation by now, you should. If you can't, in the following four-part series, *Slate* has attempted to summarize and synthesize the most controversial portions of the act so you can decide for yourself whether you want PATRIOT, and the PATRIOTs that may follow, to be a part of your world. Part 1 tackles Section 215, the law dealing with private records. Part 2 will address changes to the Foreign Intelligence

Surveillance Act, or FISA, and "sneak and peek" warrants. Part 3 will discuss new electronic surveillance, and Part 4 will discuss miscellaneous provisions, including alien detentions.

Section 215, aka "Attack of the Angry Librarians"

Section 215 is one of the surprising lightning rods of the PATRIOT Act, engendering more protest, lawsuits, and congressional amendments than any other. In part this is because this section authorizes the government to march into a library and demand a list of everyone who's ever checked out a copy of *My Secret Garden* but also because those librarians are tough.

What it does: Section 215 modifies the rules on records searches. Post–PATRIOT Act, third-party holders of your financial, library, travel, video rental, phone, medical, church, synagogue, and mosque records can be searched without your knowledge or consent, providing the government says it's trying to protect against terrorism.

The law before and how it changed: Previously the government needed at least a warrant and probable cause to access private records. The Fourth Amendment, Title III of the Omnibus Crime Control and Safe Streets Act of 1968, and case law provided that if the state wished to search you, it needed to show probable cause that a crime had been committed and to obtain a warrant from a neutral judge. Under FISA—the 1978 act authorizing warrantless surveillance so long as the primary purpose was to obtain foreign intelligence information—that was somewhat eroded, but there remained judicial oversight. And under FISA, records could be sought only "for purposes of conducting foreign intelligence" and the target "linked to foreign espionage" and an "agent of a foreign power." Now the FBI needs only to certify to a FISA judge—(no need for evidence or probable cause) that the search protects against terrorism. The judge has no authority to reject this application. DOJ calls this "seeking a court order," but it's much closer to a rubber stamp. Also, now the target of a search needn't be a terror suspect herself, so long as the government's purpose is "an authorized investigation . . . to protect against international terrorism."

Downplaying the extent of these changes, the DOJ argued to Congress that 215 is no big deal, since grand juries could always subpoena private records in the past. The difference they don't acknowledge is that investigators may now do so secretly, and these orders cannot be contested in court. While the new DOJ Web site asserts that searches under 215 are limited to "business records," the act on its face allows scrutiny of "any tangible thing" including books, records, papers, documents, and anything else. The site also says U.S. citizens may not be subject to search, but the act does not differentiate. How can it, when a library or doctor's office is simply asked to produce a list of names? And here is where the Justice Department hedges: It claims that a citizen cannot be searched *"solely on the basis of activities protected by the First Amendment to the Constitution."* That means you can't have your records searched solely because you wrote an article criticizing the PATRIOT Act. But if you are originally from India and write that article, well, that's not "solely" anymore, is it? To be sure, the ACLU is doing a bit of fearmongering when it says the DOJ can rifle through your records if they don't like what you're reading. If you're a U.S. citizen and not otherwise suspicious, you're probably safe, so long as all you do is read.

When the judiciary committee, inquiring into the civil liberties implications of PATRIOT, asked about 215, the DOJ said in July 2002: "Such an order could conceivably be served on a public library, bookstore, or newspaper, although it is unlikely that such entities maintain those types of records. If the FBI were authorized to obtain the information the more appropriate tool for requesting electronic communication transactional records would be a National Security Letter." But as we will explain in Part 4, the government's NSL authority was also beefed up by the PATRIOT

> ### *The ACLU is doing a bit of fearmongering when it says the DOJ can rifle through your records if they don't like what you're reading.*

Act. In other words, the government may simply have a more effective means of conducting warrantless searches than the one everyone's riled up about.

How it's been implemented: The DOJ is playing this one particularly close to the vest. The act itself mandates semiannual reporting by the attorney general to Congress, but the only thing he must report is the number of applications sought and granted. Not very helpful unless that number is zero. . . .

When asked by the House Committee on the Judiciary to detail whether and how many times Section 215 has been used "to obtain records from a public library, bookstore, or newspaper," the DOJ said it would send classified answers to the House Permanent Select Committee on Intelligence. The judiciary committee had what it called "reasonable limited access" to those responses, and it reported in October 2002 that its review had "not given any rise to concern that the authority is being misused or abused."

Wanting to learn more, the ACLU and some other civil rights groups filed a FOIA request, arguing that the DOJ was classifying its answers unnecessarily. But this May, a federal judge in U.S. district court in Washington ruled that the DOJ had the right to keep the specifics hush-hush under FOIA's national security exemption. The next day, at a judiciary committee hearing, Assistant Attorney General Viet Dinh did throw a bone to librarians, noting that in "an informal survey of the field offices," Justice learned "that libraries have been contacted approximately 50 times, based on articulable suspicion or voluntary calls from librarians regarding suspicious activity." He noted that most such visits were in the context of ordinary criminal investigations and did not rely on the powers granted by Section 215. He did not give specifics on searches of any other establishments.

Independent attempts to chronicle the frequency of records searches have proved inconclusive. Within months after Sept. 11, federal or local officials visited nearly 10 percent of the nation's public libraries "seeking Sept. 11–related information about patron reading habits," according to a University of Illinois survey. But since librarians are gagged under the act, it's not clear that these reports are accurate. In any event, the same study suggests that about 13.8 percent of the nation's libraries received similar requests in the year before Sept. 11, so it's impossible to say that the problem was exacerbated by the new law.

Would you know if Section 215 had been used on you?   Nope. The person made to turn over the records is gagged and cannot disclose the search to anyone.

Sunsets in 2005: Yes.

Prognosis: The first lawsuit against the PATRIOT Act was filed by the ACLU on July 30 this year, targeting Section 215. The suit has six mostly Arab and Muslim American groups as plaintiffs. Their claim is that 215 violates the Constitution and "vastly expands the power of the [FBI] to obtain records and other 'tangible things' of people not suspected of criminal activity."

In Congress, Rep. Bernard Sanders has proposed the Freedom to Read Protection Act to repeal provisions that subvert library patrons' privacy, and in July 2003 Sens. Lisa Murkowski and Ron Wyden introduced the Protecting the Rights of Individuals Act, requiring FBI agents to convince a judge of the merits of their suspicions before obtaining an individual's medical or Internet records. Similarly, Sen. Russ Feingold's Library, Bookseller and Personal Records Privacy Act would allow FBI access to business records pertaining to suspected terrorists or spies only. Feingold's bill would restore the pre-PATRIOT requirement that the FBI make a factual, individualized showing that the records sought pertain to a specific suspected terrorist.

Enough to get you through a cocktail party: 215 does extend FBI power to conduct essentially warrantless records searches, especially on people who are not themselves terror suspects, with little or no judicial oversight. The government sees this as an incremental change in the law, but the lack of meaningful judicial oversight and expanded scope of possible suspects is pretty dramatic. . . .

Part 4

Section 505, aka "National Insecurity-Complex Letters"

This section authorizes the attorney general or a delegate to compel holders of your personal records to turn them over to the government, simply by writing a "national security" letter. Section 505 has garnered a lot less national attention than Section 215—the library records section of the act—which may be why it is invoked a lot more often.

What it does: Section 505 authorizes the use of what's essentially an administrative subpoena of personal records. The subpoenas require no probable cause or judicial oversight.

The law before and how it changed: Before PATRIOT, these letters could only be issued against individuals who were reasonably suspected of espionage. But PATRIOT loosened the standard by allowing the letters to be used against anyone, including U.S. citizens, even if they themselves are not suspected of espionage or criminal activity. These letters may now be issued independently by FBI field offices, rather than by senior officials. And unlike Section 215 warrants, they are not subject to even perfunctory judicial review or oversight.

The records that can be obtained through the letters under PATRIOT include telephone logs, e-mail logs, certain financial and bank records, and credit reports, on the assertion that such information would be "relevant" to an ongoing terrorism investigation. They cannot be used in ordinary criminal investigations. Unlike 215, no court order—not even a rubber-stamped order—is required. Those forced to turn over records are gagged from disclosing the demand.

How it's been implemented: According to documents turned over to the American Civil Liberties Union as part of their FOIA lawsuit, the FBI issued enough national security letters since October 2001 to fill more than five pages of logs. What precisely those letters compelled is unknowable, since virtually every page of those logs were blacked out, ostensibly for security reasons. The government has refused to provide further information on how the letters were used.

A November 2001 memorandum prepared by FBI attorneys warned that the letters "must be used judiciously" to appease Congress, since they expire in 2005, along with other PATRIOT provisions.

Would you know if Section 505 had been used on you: Not unless some action was brought against you based on the information produced.

Sunsets in 2005: Yes.

Prognosis: Sen. Barbara Boxer, D-Calif., introduced the Library and Bookseller Protection Act, S 1158, in May 2003, which exempts libraries and booksellers from having to produce records pursuant to National Security letters. The Protecting the Rights of Individuals Act, S 1552, introduced by Sens. Lisa Murkowski, R-Alaska, and Ron Wyden, D-Ore., does the same thing.

Enough to get you through a cocktail party: While few Americans seem to be getting exercised over Section 505, it's actually a good deal scarier than 215—the angry librarian provision—in some ways. Why? Because there is no check on the attorney general's discretion, not even a toothless judge. Add to this the government's refusal to disclose how these letters have been used, and there are some grounds for paranoia over this provision.

Section 802, aka "Tree-Hugging Terrorists"

This section has received a lot of attention and is almost single-handedly responsible for alienating right-wing groups like the Eagle Forum, as well as fundamentalist Christians across the land. Why? Because it creates a new crime and could, critics say, be used someday to prosecute Operation Rescue protesters.

What it does: Section 802 creates a category of crime called "domestic terrorism," penalizing activities that "involve acts dangerous to human life that are a violation of the criminal laws of the United States," if the actor's intent is to "influence the policy of a government by intimidation or coercion."

The law before and how it changed: There was no law like this before.

How it's been implemented: The ACLU has conceded that despite the scary hypothetical applications, it knows of no abortion protester or environmental activist who has been prosecuted under the law.

Would you know if Section 802 had been used on you: You'd likely figure it out right quick as they were hauling you away in handcuffs.

Sunsets in 2005: Yes.

Prognosis: The Murkowski and Wyden Protecting the Rights of Individuals Act would narrow the definition of "terrorism," so the law's expanded enforcement tools could not be used against domestic political protesters.

Enough to get you through a cocktail party: The fears over this provision are almost entirely hypothetical. Maybe Greenpeace activists really are on the hook, but that sounds a bit overheated in light of the text of the act. And while fearmongers in the press have suggested that you can now be jailed for a bar fight, the statute requires both endangering of life and an intent to influence the government. This provision is more bark than bite.

Sections 411 and 412, aka "Alien and Sedition Acts"

It's important to note from the outset that virtually all of the administration's unprecedented abuse of aliens—the indefinite detentions, the blanket secrecy, the lack of charges, and the removal of aliens to secret military brigs—have happened absent any legislative authority. While some provisions of PATRIOT make it easier for the government to treat aliens poorly, PATRIOT in no way authorized the worst reported abuses.

What they do: Section 411 makes even unknowing association with terrorists a deportable offense. Section 412 allows the attorney general to order a brief detention of aliens without any prior showing or court ruling that the person is dangerous.

The law before and how it changed: 411 makes aliens deportable for associating, even unknowingly, with a "terrorist organization." 412 gives the attorney general new power to order detentions based on a certification that he has "reasonable grounds to believe" that a noncitizen endangers national security. No judicial review is provided except for habeas corpus—a most basic and unlikely avenue of appeal. And the attorney general may continue to hold the alien indefinitely. If an alien does not have a country willing to accept him, he may now be detained indefinitely without trial. Moreover, the act allows for aliens to be held for seven days without being charged with a crime. The act requires a biannual report to Congress but the report need not contain information including the names of those held, when they were seized, where they were detained, or the nature of the charges against them.

How it's been implemented: Sparingly. The DOJ noted in May that the INS has denied admission to all of three aliens (including one who was believed to be a money-launderer) on the security grounds expanded in Section 411. As for Section 412, it hadn't yet been used as of March.

Which is not to say that the INS hasn't detained, deported, or denied admission to bushels of aliens since Sept. 11. But it's generally a big old hassle to deport someone on "security-related" grounds like the ones expanded in Section 411. As the DOJ gingerly put it in May, "security-related grounds of removal may generate more litigation." Through March, every time the INS deported an alien it wasn't keen on, it did so on non-security-related grounds to expedite the removal. Still, the DOJ would like this sunsetted provision to stick around in case any terrorists show up with their visas in perfect order.

> *Americans have begun to demand that the freedoms we surrender correspond directly to national security.*

Would you know if Sections 411 and 412 had been used on you: Well, if you're one of those three excluded aliens, you're probably aware that you're not in the United States right now. Otherwise, it hasn't.

Sunsets in 2005: Yes for both.

Enough to get you through a cocktail party: These provisions, permitting possibly lengthy detentions based on little more than a John Ashcroft sniff test, would be far more disturbing if aliens weren't subject to far worse abuses at the hands of the administration.

Conclusion:

In studying and reporting on the most controversial aspects of the PATRIOT Act, we have attempted to be as evenhanded as possible. It bears repeating that the Bush administration has fostered a good deal of national anxiety by its simple refusal to release information allaying public fears about how the act is being implemented.

Immediately after Sept. 11, many Americans seemed to fall victim to an understandable fallacy: We believed that by surrendering our freedoms, we were buying national security. Slowly the haze of fear has cleared, and Americans have begun to demand that the freedoms we surrender correspond directly to national security. The parts of the PATRIOT Act that rankle most are those provisions that sweep normal criminal law enforcement under the looser procedural standards for fighting terror. It's important that the state be able to fight terror. No one disputes this. But it's equally important that the state not use the war on terror to gut the warrant requirement or undermine the First Amendment.

The best check on such encroachments should be a free and objective judiciary. But as we have noted several times in this series, many of the most disturbing PATRIOT provisions do away with judicial oversight altogether, while others permit judges to act as rubber stamps in *ex parte* proceedings—that is, hearings where only the government side is represented.

The next best check on such encroachments is public scrutiny, and, as we've suggested, that scrutiny is only beginning to be as demanding and impatient as it ought. But most Americans still do not believe that PATRIOT has in any way affected them. So it's worth noting that many of these provisions are used frequently—even if details are blacked out. Go back and look at the sections that ask whether you'd know if PATRIOT has been used against you. In most cases the answer is no.

We really can be safe without being afraid of our government. It simply requires that security measures be narrowly tailored to fit national security needs. Some parts of the USA PATRIOT Act meet this test. Some do not. And some are purely opportunistic. Before President Bush convinces Congress to "untie the hands of our law enforcement officials" by expanding the PATRIOT Act, as he proposed Wednesday, Americans need to begin a national conversation about which is which.

IV. Immigration and Border Patrols

Editors' Introduction

T he United States has about 12,383 miles of coastline, on the Atlantic, the Pacific, the Arctic, and the Gulf, and about 7,500 miles of land border, much of it through rugged terrain. The border with Mexico is about 2,000 miles long and traverses some forbidding deserts; the border between Canada and the lower 48 states is about 4,000 miles long, much of it cut through deep forest; and the border between Canada and Alaska accounts for another 1,500 miles, probably the roughest of all. Across these borders noncitizens stream, making about 350 million visits to the United States each year for the purposes of trade, tourism, work, education, and settlement.

Traditionally the United States has been hospitable to visitors and immigrants, but 9/11 altered that. It sparked fears that terrorists would enter the country undetected, using false papers or contracting help from the criminal networks that regularly smuggle contraband and people over the borders (and sometimes far into the interior—a security agent's nightmare). Post–9/11, the U.S. government is making a serious attempt to keep track of all the foreign nationals who enter the country at established crossing points. A plan to check in visitors, with fingerprints and photographs, when they arrive and check them out when they leave is progressing slowly, but this does not deal with the problem of covert entry. To address that issue, the government has strengthened law enforcement along both borders, hiring additional personnel and adopting more aggressive tactics.

Although the Canadian border is twice as long as the border with Mexico, it is not half so closely guarded. Long stretches are not patrolled at all. In "The Big Bad Border," from the *Seattle Weekly*, Nina Shapiro explains why the U.S. authorities are suddenly paying attention to the longest undefended border in the world and how difficult it may be to police, even with help from the Canadian Mounties.

At the southern border federal agents claim that they have captured smugglers who are moving Middle Easterners into the United States, Bruce Finley reports in the *Denver Post* ("Migrant Smugglers Traffic in Terror, Federal Officials Say"). However, these arrests, which the government will not discuss in any detail, have been accompanied by a decline in arrests for the ordinary immigration violations that are often committed by Latino illegals and their American employers. Some critics think the immigration authorities may be overreacting to the threat of infiltration and assigning resources to the "war on terror" that are still needed for conventional duties.

In "Anti-terrorism Plans Stall," from the *Detroit News*, Brad Heath describes programs for monitoring legal visitors and checking up on foreign students to see that they do not overstay their visas or violate their terms of admission.

These programs, which were authorized well before 9/11 but not funded until afterwards, will in time give the government a much better idea of who the foreign nationals are in the United States, where they are staying, and what they are doing. At present, however, the effort is running somewhat behind schedule, slowed by the massive amounts of data that must be absorbed and plagued by computer glitches.

Not all immigrants are here legally, of course. The government would like to locate and expel those who have overstayed their visas or committed more serious crimes and, most important, identify any who may have ties to terrorist groups. The Justice Department and immigration authorities conducted "sweeps" of Muslim and Middle Eastern immigrants after 9/11 and held many people in custody. Now an internal report by the department's own inspector general has revealed some serious abuse of detainees. "Report on PATRIOT Act Alleges Rights Violations," from the *Newsletter on Intellectual Freedom*, provides the details of these cases.

Perhaps in response to such revelations, the Department of Homeland Security discontinued, after much criticism, a special registration program for immigrants from countries that were thought to be harboring terrorists. The program had been initiated by the Justice Department in 2002, before Homeland Security took over matters of immigration. While it was in effect, approximately 83,000 male immigrants from Muslim nations came to government offices to register and be fingerprinted; almost 14,000 were then immediately detained or placed in deportation proceedings, principally because their papers were not in order. Several dozen criminals were also discovered, but only seven men who could be suspected of possible terrorist connections (as yet no charges have been filed). In early December 2003, the Homeland Security Department decided that the voluntary registration program was not an effective weapon against terrorists or a sensible use of resources and abandoned it altogether; the program had become a political and diplomatic liability, triggering protests at home and abroad.

How heightened security may affect foreign students and professors, as well as the American universities where they work, is the subject of Madhusree Mukerjee's "Boxed Out," from *Scientific American*. American programs in chemistry, physics, microbiology, and advanced technology draw heavily on foreign talent, but scholars are finding it much harder to get permission to study or conduct research in the United States, possibly because of confusion, in overseas consulates, as to what constitutes a "sensitive field." Remembering the contributions that foreigners have made to American science and defense in the past, Mukerjee speculates on the long-term effects of the present chill.

The Big Bad Border[1]

By Nina Shapiro
Seattle Weekly, September 10, 2003

One chilly day in late February, Costa Rican native Marvin Navarro-Ortiz set out to sneak into the United States. His attempted point of entry was the heavily wooded and treacherously rocky Vedder Mountain, which straddles the U.S.–Canadian border among the quiet rural towns just north of Bellingham.

The 35-year-old had been living legally in Toronto for the past six months, working construction and odd jobs, according to his girlfriend, Rachel Gazzillo, an American who lives in Costa Rica. But Gazzillo says he knew he could make more money in the States, where he had lived for 12 years previously, much of it on the East Coast working in a satellite-dish factory. He had sent money home to support his impoverished mother. Having recently gone home to see his family, he looked for a way to get back to the U.S. In Canada, his girlfriend says, Navarro-Ortiz found "coyotes" who offered him a choice: a smuggling route across the eastern border for $3,000, or one across the western one for $1,500.

"We were all very worried that something bad was going to happen," Gazzillo says, speaking by telephone from San Jose, Costa Rica. "The borders are being guarded more closely now. We didn't want him to get caught or wind up in prison—or worse."

Their fears were well founded. Navarro-Ortiz and a compatriot apparently got lost on Vedder Mountain. Losing his footing, Navarro-Ortiz dropped some 100 feet to the rocky base of a waterfall. By the time a search-and-rescue team made it up there on Feb. 27, responding to a resident's call about persistent yelling on the mountain, Navarro-Ortiz was dead.

The case was unusual only in that it had turned fatal. Every year, thousands of people try to sneak into the U.S. from Canada. The latest prominent case was that of two Pakistani men arrested last month at Seattle-Tacoma International Airport, one of whom was on a federal "no-fly" list for uncertain reasons, after they were smuggled across the border on foot.

The northern border has long been ignored as public attention has been riveted on the southern border, a place of mythological stature in the American psyche, where our expansionist history confronts the economic desperation of our neighbors and the seemingly unstoppable flood of illicit migration. Attention began turning to the Canadian border, however, in the winter of 1999, when

---

1. Article by Nina Shapiro from *Seattle Weekly* September 10, 2003. Copyright © *Seattle Weekly*. Reprinted with permission.

authorities caught would-be Islamic terrorist Ahmed Ressam entering at Port Angeles with a trunkload of explosives. At a congressional hearing shortly after, Rep. Lamar Smith, R-Texas, warned that "terrorists, and also illegal aliens, alien smugglers, and drug smugglers, are increasingly using Canada as a transit country en route to the United States."

In the post–9/11 era of homeland security, there have been more congressional hearings on the subject, which has become enough a part of the public consciousness that the TV show *West Wing* had an episode based on terrorists arriving from Canada. Suddenly, the nation has become acutely aware of its vulnerability from the "world's longest undefended border"—5,200 miles of mountains, wilderness, waterways, and mostly unfenced land, with law-enforcement officers few and far between. Until recently, only some 300 Border Patrol agents were assigned to the northern border, in contrast to the approximately 9,000 guarding the 2,000 miles on the southern border with Mexico.

The Canadian border "was more than undefended—it was wide open," says Tom Hardy, head of the Seattle office of the federal

---

"It's almost like we've been Mexicanizing the Canadian border."—Deborah Meyers, policy analyst at the Migration Policy Institute

---

Bureau of Customs and Border Protection, part of the newly created Department of Homeland Security.

In response, Congress voted to triple the previously paltry number of agents on the northern border. By the end of the year, the northern border is supposed to be guarded by 375 more agents—the largest northern deployment in the Border Patrol's history and one that will achieve its goal of having 1,000 officers from Blaine to Maine.

"It's almost like we've been Mexicanizing the Canadian border," says Deborah Meyers, a prominent policy analyst at the Migration Policy Institute. That doesn't trouble Meyers, who, like many, believes that "we've never funded the Canadian border in the way in which it needs to be funded." But Bellingham immigration attorney Greg Boos detects a note of aggression in the growing rhetoric over the Canadian border that has him wondering whether the government might move toward the kind of paramilitary presence on the northern border that it has on the southern. Such a strategy would not go over well in his parts, he says. "We consider ourselves to be friends of Canada up here."

Nor, Boos argues, would it be effective. "The Mexican model doesn't work on the Mexican border, so why would it work on the Canadian border?" It's a question you hear again and again from a wide array of people concerned, including other immigration attorneys, policy analysts, and law-enforcement officers in both the U.S.

and Canada. It arises not only because the U.S. is beefing up its law-enforcement presence along the Canadian border but because it is doing so in a way that accords with a strategy developed on the Mexican border. Called "forward deployment," it stresses having agents in highly visible positions right on the border, a policy aimed at deterring illegal entry but one that critics feel neglects important investigative work and enforcement efforts inside the country.

Meanwhile, the new emphasis on the Canadian border has irritated some of our northern neighbors at a time when relations already are strained over differing stands on the war against terrorism. "Everyone is aware—at least in Canada—that the terrorists who perpetrated the attacks against the World Trade Center didn't enter from Canada," says Elizabeth Bryson, an immigration attorney in Vancouver, B.C. "Yet what's the immediate reaction? Blame it on Canada." Some hasten to add that the border problem, contrary to how Americans are accustomed to thinking, works both ways, with illicit activity coming from, as well as into, the U.S.

The border problem . . . works both ways,
with illicit activity coming from, as well as
into, the U.S.

It Cuts Both Ways

Carey James arrived at the northern border in 1996 to take over the Border Patrol's Blaine sector, which runs from the ocean to the Cascades. Like most people in the Border Patrol, who are required to start their career on the Mexican border and to speak Spanish, James had what he calls a "southern border mentality. The idea was that coming up here was a vacation. All of a sudden, I'm here, and it's—whoa, buddy."

Unquestionably, Border Patrol agents on the southern border face a far greater influx of people. For the 10-month period ending July 31, the Border Patrol arrested 8,170 people on the northern border and 748,403 people on the southern border. (Those numbers are somewhat deceiving because the paucity of agents on the northern border leads them to catch what they suspect is a small fraction of the illegal traffic, but they give some perspective.) The northern border, however, is a more complicated place, contends James, who retired from the Border Patrol two years ago and now serves as undersheriff of Whatcom County. Whereas most everyone trying to get in from the south is from Mexico or neighboring countries, James says, "up here, it's not unusual to get 30 or 40 different ethnic groups in a month." And they're coming to the U.S. for a variety of reasons.

First, there's the drug trade. "B.C. bud" is the nickname for the marijuana grown in British Columbia—usually indoors using artificial light that yields an extremely potent product. It is considered some of the best marijuana in the world, and Canadian authorities believe it is grown in large part for Americans. Over the past decade, it has become the third- or fourth-biggest industry in British Columbia. Last year, U.S. authorities seized almost 28,000 pounds of marijuana at the border. So valuable is the product, police think, that sometimes it is sold pound for pound for cocaine—the primary drug that the United States sends into Canada. Police there seized 350 pounds of coke at the border last year. The players in the cross-border drug trade are a mix, but at least some of the coke dealers come from the Colombian and other Latin American cartels that traverse the U.S., while Vietnamese immigrants and the Hell's Angels are active in the Canadian marijuana scene.

The Ressam case and our new focus on border security have made Canada's asylum policies the subject of a furious controversy.

Human smuggling across the northern border into the U.S. is also big business. The $1,500 reportedly paid by Navarro-Ortiz seems to have been a bargain. Joe Giullano, an assistant chief of the Border Patrol's Blaine sector, says smugglers charge as much as $15,000 per person. Some of those trips, though, originate in the person's home country, with smugglers providing false documents as they usher their clients onto airplanes to Canada, where they then arrange for a land crossing into the U.S.

The choice of Canada as an entry point to the U.S. might be due to visa and immigration policies there. Costa Ricans like Navarro-Ortiz, for instance, don't need visas to visit Canada, nor do Mexicans or Koreans. Korean smuggling operations are some of the biggest currently seen at the border. The Canadian process of requesting asylum also makes it easier for foreigners to live in Canada legally, at least temporarily, than to do so in the U.S. Unlike here, Canada requires no initial screening of asylum applicants to determine whether they have a credible claim of persecution. Applicants are allowed to live in Canada until they have a hearing, a time period that currently runs at about a year. Navarro-Ortiz was living in Canada as an asylum seeker, though his girlfriend knows of no persecution he was suffering. So was Algerian terrorist Ressam.

The Ressam case and our new focus on border security have made Canada's asylum policies the subject of a furious controversy. U.S. officials have expressed concern about what they perceive as a lax policy, and some prominent Canadians have backed them up. "Anybody can claim to be persecuted and we'll let them in," complains James Bissett, a retired director of the Canadian Immigration Service (now called Citizenship and Immigration Canada), speaking by phone from Ottawa. "We'll allow them to work while they wait for a hearing, and if they're unable to find work, we'll give them full welfare benefits and free legal advice." When it comes to people looking for asylum, he says, Canada has become "the country of choice," drawing immigrants from, among other places, Yemen, Saudi Arabia, and Libya—"countries that we know produce terrorists."

Dave Harris, a former chief of strategic planning for the Canadian Security Intelligence Service (CSIS) and now the president of a consulting firm focusing on security, echoes the sentiment: "If you were a terrorist infiltrator, you'd be guilty of negligence by not taking advantage of our refugee system."

Canada has been pumping billions of dollars into its own antiterrorism efforts since 9/11 and has pledged to ramp up the screening of refugee applicants as well as visitors. It's worth noting that, notwithstanding its tougher asylum process, the United States probably has at least as big a problem with terrorist infiltration as does Canada. "With the possible exception of the United States, there are more international terrorist organizations active in Canada than anywhere in the world," reads a CSIS report. One primary reason CSIS gives for this situation: "Canada's proximity to the United States." In other words, many of the terrorists are only in Canada because it's a handy point for getting to us. Our problem becomes their problem.

Yet, as in the U.S., some in Canada believe those on the antiterrorist bandwagon are exaggerating the problem to further anti-immigration policies. That doesn't sit well with Canadians who see their country as being the true land of immigrants, and the U.S., for all its welcoming rhetoric, as being hostile to immigrants, particularly those who are Muslim and non-European. "Our immigration policy differs from the U.S. in one sense: It's very positive," says Martin Rudner, a professor of international affairs at Carleton University in Ottawa. "We want 1 percent of our population to be immigrants every year—that's a strategy." So when the U.S. suggests that Canada tighten up its immigration policies—even if some within Canada are in full agreement—it's taken as an attack on Canadian values, not to mention its sovereignty. "The U.S. government would like to dictate to Canada its immigration policies and standards," says Vancouver immigration attorney Bryson.

All the while, complain some, Americans take no responsibility for the cross-border security problem posed by laws that Canadians consider lax—namely our gun laws. In Canada, everyone who buys a gun has to take a firearms-safety course, apply for a license, and register the gun's serial number with the government. The process can take months. Only individuals who belong to gun clubs can buy handguns, and even then, they must be transported in a locked box, in the trunk of a car. Thus has developed the market for illegal guns smuggled in from the U.S., where waiting periods are days, not months, and few other regulations exist.

"It's a huge problem," says Wendy Cukier, president of Canada's Coalition for Gun Control and a professor of justice studies at Ryerson University in Toronto. "At least half of the handguns recovered in crime in Canada have been smuggled in from the U.S." Just last year, Canadian authorities seized more than 5,000 firearms at the border.

Consequently, while some in Canada bristle at American talk of building up enforcement on the border, others couldn't agree more and, in fact, worry about the discussions of "open borders" that were until recently in vogue. "Strengthening, not relaxing, border controls is needed," proclaims a position paper of the Coalition for Gun Control. The Canadian Police Association has taken the same position, noting both the drug and gun traffic as well as the odd American fugitive who sneaks into Canada hoping to escape punishment.

In Search of Lizard Men

"This is the border right here," says Kerri Hunter, supervisor of a Border Patrol unit based in the town of Lynden. It's dusk, and we're in his truck, bumping up and down on a dirt road that is, literally, the border. On either side of us are the raspberry fields that are the dominant crop on the modest farms that lie below the mountains. To the untrained eye, there is absolutely no indication that one side is Canada, the other the U.S.—no checkpoints, no markers, no fences. As Hunter drives along, noting light patches in the soil that might represent unlawful foot traffic, he discloses the presence of ground sensors at locations he can't name. Nearby, too, are cameras on towering silver poles with which the Border Patrol dotted the landscape after 9/11. Still, the dense rows of raspberry plants, which grow to about 4 feet tall, call out as the perfect cover for someone who wants to crouch their way across the border.

It's hard to imagine an easier route—until you drive along a legendary road known as Boundary Avenue, which, true to its name, runs exactly along the border, traveling east from Lynden. Across a grassy median spanning a few feet is an equally legendary Canadian road called 0 Avenue (that's "zero"). "All it takes are two cars on either side and a couple of cell phones," says Hunter. "Hey, I'm here. I don't see anybody." The person on one side can throw a hockey bag full of drugs to the other or can tell a load of immigrants to scramble across, and the car waiting on the other side can zoom off. "They're on pavement already," Hunter says. The exchange takes seconds. A few weeks prior to my visit, a smuggler tried to get a dozen Koreans across in a camper shell attached to a pickup truck, which simply swerved off 0 and onto Boundary. The Border Patrol saw this group on camera and arrested them as they were attempting their getaway.

Across the border a couple weeks later, Sgt. Gerry Freill of the Royal Canadian Mounted Police (RCMP) takes me to a swath of 0 Avenue farther west, juxtaposed not with Boundary Avenue but a patch of woods. There he points out a wryly amusing symbol of the ease with which the border is crossed—an international marker with an illicit foot path running brazenly right by it. "The smugglers use them as landmarks," Freill says of the little cone-shaped markers.

Freill runs a branch of an award-winning Mounties team that works with various law-enforcement agencies on both sides of the border to stop illicit traffic, called the Integrated Border Enforcement Team, or IBET. Working undercover in jeans, out of a blue pickup truck that serves as his office, the gray-haired and deceptively easy-going Freill is eager to talk about the border problem. He drives to another point on 0 Avenue, bordered by woods on the American side and by an open field on the Canadian side that gently slopes down to a golf course. One night last February, the Border Patrol, using an infrared camera, picked up three men headed into Canada at this spot. The Americans alerted the RCMP, whose officers chased after the guys until they found them hiding in a creek near the golf course. Dressed in camouflage gear, they were sporting backpacks containing 41 guns, two machine pistols, and $100,000 U.S.

The ringleader belonged to a Seattle street gang, according to Freill, and also was "a known pimp. He's got a number of working girls he runs up and down the West Coast. In addition to that, he's involved in the gun trade. So he collects handguns and sells them to organized crime groups here." With the profits, Freill believes he used to buy B.C. bud and take it back south, which might explain why he and his cohorts had some extra cash on hand.

Traveling on to a nearby swamp, Freill recalls one of the most memorable busts he ever made, of another American who tried to sneak into Canada with some ready cash. "We call him Lizard Man." The Mounties caught him several years back walking through the swamp, water up to his shoulders. He was wearing a wet suit under military fatigues and night-vision goggles on his painted face. He carried thousands of U.S. dollars in a pack on the back of his neck.

Easy as it is to hop across the border at some points, some people figure they'll have even less chance of being caught in more out-of-the-way spots. "It just goes to show you the length they will go to," Freill says.

That's true for people coming our way, too, of course, as demonstrated by Navarro-Ortiz and an arrest made by Freill in December. He caught three Canadians heading up a steep mountain path into the U.S. on snowshoes, their backpacks filled with B.C. bud.

The question is, what to do about it? The Canadian border is a problem but not anywhere near the problem that is the Mexican border. And yet, it takes only one terrorist to capitalize on undeniably easy access to cause us major harm. There have been two known cases of terrorists trying to do so: Ressam, who had planned to bomb Los Angeles International Airport, and lesser-known Abu Mezer. Caught three times trying to sneak in from Canada, Mezer, a Palestinian, somehow was released and made it to New York, where, in 1997, he was arrested before carrying out a planned suicide bombing on the subway. So how far do we go in erecting barriers to a country that is, mostly, a political ally and our No. 1 trading partner?

Officially, authorities stress that there has to be balance. "Essentially, a large part of the free world's economy is in your hands," says Border Patrol Assistant Chief Joe Giullano. "Do you really want to shut down the border?" The 2001 Smart Border Declaration, negotiated by U.S. Homeland Security Director Tom Ridge and then–Foreign Minister John Manley of Canada, emphasizes cooperation and intelligence sharing between the two countries and developing common databases and even some joint inspection facilities. "You have to look at the ability to work with the Canadians as opposed to setting up a line of defense at the 49th Parallel," says Freill of the Mounties.

Yet Freill is one of a number of people who wonder whether the Border Patrol is trying to do just that with its strategy of forward deployment. It's a strategy that began in El Paso, Texas, in the

---

How far do we go in erecting barriers to a country that is, mostly, a political ally and our No. 1 trading partner?

---

early '90s, then dubbed Operation Hold the Line, and moved west to San Diego. The idea was to deter illegal immigration by creating a human wall of Border Patrol agents, who kept watch in trucks stationed every quarter-mile or so. At first the results seemed dramatic. Apprehensions plummeted in El Paso and elsewhere. But the consensus among leading thinkers on the border is that the strategy eventually proved a failure. Much of the illicit traffic just moved to the southwestern desert, where those who didn't perish in the crossing were likely to encounter less law enforcement. "The bottom line is that there is as much illegal immigration as there was 10 years ago and as much [smuggled] drugs as there were 10 years ago," says Stephen Flynn, a senior fellow at the Council on Foreign Relations and a retired Coast Guard commander.

Forward deployment took hold up north two years ago, when Ronald Henley became chief of the Border Patrol's Blaine sector. It's a modified version of the strategy, explains Henley, who wrote the plan for the entire northern border while serving in the Border Patrol's California-based Western headquarters. Even with the tripling of agents, he says, the Border Patrol won't have enough manpower to form a line across 5,200 miles. The northern strategy is more "intelligence-driven," he says.

But deterrence through the high visibility of agents is still the cornerstone of the strategy. And that means agents have in large part stopped doing other work, such as raids on logging camps and farms and jail checks to determine whether suspects are illegal immigrants. (Homeland Security's Bureau of Immigration and Customs Enforcement, or ICE, is now responsible for interior enforcement, but it's unclear how much of the Border Patrol's former work it will pick up.) Despite the talk of cross-border cooperation, the Blaine sector also has scaled down its work with the Canadian IBET team, no longer assigning any dedicated agents to the effort.

"It's horribly boring," Daryl Schermerhorn, a Lynden agent and vice president of the national Border Patrol union, says of the new mandate. "How many circles can you drive? We're tripping over each other at the border when we could be doing all this other stuff."

Not all critics of the policy would like to see more draconian raids on immigrant workplaces; some, in fact, would like to see hard-working illegal immigrants legalized so that border authorities can focus on people who mean to do us harm. But many agree that agents don't have time for critical intelligence gathering if they've got their "butt parked in a truck" at the border, as Kathleen Walker, a longtime immigration attorney in El Paso, puts it. Instead, she says, agents should "try to track down smuggling rings and put them out of business."

Former Blaine Border Patrol chief James and his retired deputy, Eugene Davis, sitting in Davis' Bellingham house, further argue that vital information comes from catching bad guys through strategic operations rather than merely trying to deter them. That gives authorities a chance to interrogate transgressors and use subsequent information to trace problems back to the source. "If the guy is a terrorist, you're much better off catching him and finding out who he is and what he is," Davis says. Especially, he and James add, because terrorists and other criminals will inevitably find a way across a vast border that is impossible to seal off. "If you're a terrorist intent on coming to this country, [forward deployment] will just push you to another area where you can do harm," James says, citing the example of what happened on the Mexican border.

"Nowhere in the Border Patrol handbook does it say to allow people into the country so you can talk to them," counters Chief Henley. "You don't allow someone into the country with a nuclear weapon so you can chat."

Still, deterrence has been shown to be unachievable on the Mexican border and has even less chance of being effective on the longer and more open Canadian border. So how reassuring is the Border Patrol's new visibility? It might have a role, but it might also be creating the illusion of control—what immigration attorney Walker, among others, calls an "optical" solution. Concludes Meyers of the Migration Policy Institute: "A lot of the most important measures are ones that are not visible."

Migrant Smugglers Traffic in Terror, Federal Officials Say[2]

By Bruce Finley
The Denver Post, September 14, 2003

Federal agents are investigating whether smuggling networks that traditionally helped illegal workers enter the United States are now being used to smuggle terrorists, officials have told *The Denver Post*.

High-ranking agents say the U.S.–Mexico border still is vulnerable to smuggling, that possible terrorist traffic may flow through Colorado, and that smugglers are enticed by huge potential profits from terrorist clients as legal entry becomes more difficult.

Smuggling groups based in the Middle East and Asia "are teaming up with traditional Latin American organizations to help move their cargo into the United States," said Jim Chaparro, special agent in charge of U.S. Immigration and Customs Enforcement across a four-state region that includes Colorado. Chaparro formerly ran anti-smuggling investigations nationwide.

"These guys are playing hardball, the terrorists," Chaparro said. "They are never going to quit."

The mobilization against smuggling of what the government calls "special interest aliens" reflects new priorities as duties of the former Immigration and Naturalization Service fall to the Department of Homeland Security and ICE, the agency's investigative arm.

ICE chiefs refer to numerous arrests. But officials would not discuss what evidence they had in smuggling cases that involve links to suspected terrorist groups, saying that classified intelligence would compromise current operations.

That is raising concerns from advocacy groups about civil liberties and traditional enforcement of immigration laws.

While agents focus on cases with possible national security implications—also increasing scrutiny of visitors from predominantly Muslim countries and of all foreign students—they are posting sharply diminished results in enforcement of laws against illegal immigrant labor.

A *Denver Post* review of the government's latest immigration data found:

- Fewer immigrant arrests: Investigators charged with arresting illegal immigrants inside the United States found fewer from 2000 to 2002–41 percent fewer nationwide, 21 percent fewer in the region, and 43 percent fewer in Southwest border sectors.

  The new national security emphasis means fewer agents are available for traditional immigration enforcement, Homeland Security officials said. Officials also theorize that stricter border control and a lagging economy could be deterring would-be migrants.

  The latest U.S. Census Bureau estimates, however, show a record 8 million illegal immigrants in the United States, increasing at the rate of 500,000 a year.

- Workplace warnings halved: The number of U.S. employers warned or cited for knowingly hiring illegal workers decreased by more than 50 percent during the same period. Investigators say that's because they are concentrating on employers at airports and utilities deemed critical for national security.

- Decrease in smuggler arrests: Enforcement targeting traditional smuggling, primarily of illegal workers from Mexico and Central America, resulted in 19 percent fewer arrests of smugglers and 58 percent fewer arrests of smuggled illegal workers.

- More deportations of Muslims: In contrast, deportations of immigrants from 15 predominantly Muslim countries such as Pakistan, Egypt and Jordan increased by 85 percent from 2000 to 2002. "We try to posture our enforcement resources with where we see the greatest threat. We think we are doing what is prudent, proper and most effective," said Chuck DeMore, ICE assistant director for investigations in Washington. "We will continue to posture ourselves as we are presently, as long as we see the threats as we see them now."

Current operations against smugglers suspected of moving Middle Easterners into the United States are based on classified intelligence. "There's no way we can tell you publicly what we are doing to counter that," ICE spokesman Chris Bentley said, "because that would jeopardize any operation that we are trying to undertake."

Revamp Doubles Force

The breakup of the INS and its merger with Homeland Security this year were designed to boost communication among multiple intelligence agencies. The restructuring increased the INS force of 2,000 investigators by pulling in customs and money-laundering agents to create an unprecedented force of 5,000 Homeland Security special agents.

They are deployed, based on daily threat assessments, to anything from tracking foreign students to countersmuggling operations. The latest ICE budget tops $2.4 billion, part of the overall $41 billion devoted to Homeland Security.

ICE chiefs cited a handful of arrests over the past two years as evidence that their countersmuggling efforts are warranted:

- In January 2002, ICE agents arrested Iranian Mohammed Assadi in Miami after Colombian authorities arrested him for encouraging several Iraqis to enter the United States.

    ICE's Chaparro said: "Assadi was the head of a major smuggling organization that operated out of Ecuador, Colombia and the Caribbean. His smuggling network was responsible for the illegal entry of hundreds of Middle Eastern aliens into the United States."

    The status of the case is unclear; Assadi was acquitted of some charges last year.

- That same month, ICE agents in Miami arrested Mehrzad Arbane, another accused smuggler, after authorities in Ecuador caught him with cocaine and expelled him to the United States to face criminal smuggling charges. Now jailed in New York, Arbane is suspected of running a smuggling organization that moved migrants from Iraq, Iran, Syria and Jordan to the United States.

    "There's no evidence of (smuggling)," said his attorney, Thomas O'Hern.

- In December, ICE agents in San Diego arrested Salim Boughader, a Mexican of Lebanese descent. Chaparro said Boughader ran a global organization that specialized in moving special interest aliens via Lebanon to the United States. In March, Boughader pleaded guilty to running a group that brought more than 100 mostly Lebanese immigrants into San Diego. He was sentenced to a year in prison in a deal that avoided a trial.

- On August 26, Khaled Abukasem, 28, a Syrian-born Palestinian who was in the United States illegally, violating the terms of a student visa, pleaded guilty in Texas to illegal possession of a gun. Abukasem told federal agents that he was recruited by the Palestine Liberation Organization, trained as a fighter pilot and enrolled in flight lessons in the United States, according to federal prosecutors in Houston.

- An investigation of Muhammad Wazen Ahmad Jarad alleged that he was a large-scale smuggler of Middle Easterners, predominantly from Iraq. Chaparro said: "Jarad had worked closely with Assadi's smuggling organization and provided valuable testimony against Assadi at his trial."

But there was no proof linking these men to specific groups that the U.S. government associates with terrorism.

And revealing more information about these and other cases could prompt enemies to change their tactics before they are caught, said Joe Greene, ICE deputy assistant director of investigations.

These arrests "are of guys responsible for moving hundreds of people into the United States, some of whom may pose a threat to us," Greene said.

Several Probes in Progress

ICE agents said several investigations into smuggling of Middle Easterners are in progress, including at least one case with Colorado connections. They are scrutinizing rival gangs in the Phoenix area that run a network of safe houses and transit routes across the country.

A pattern is emerging, said ICE Special Agent Mike McMahon, a 29-year INS veteran based in Houston.

> *"Even the most basic functions of immigration enforcement are being abandoned to focus almost exclusively on national security."*—**Steven Camarota, Center for Immigration Studies**

Smugglers in search of profits—knowing agents are especially watchful of people from predominantly Muslim countries—set up bases in countries with which their home countries have visa-waiver or trade treaties. Colombia and Ecuador have emerged as key bases.

"They enter that country, usually legitimately, as a visitor," McMahon said. From there, they link with existing regional smuggling networks to move migrants "through the waterways, air routes and land routes" into the United States.

"They associate and do business with one another. They pursue different corridors. They transit different areas. We have a number of targets identified in Cuba."

The 1,952-mile U.S. border with Mexico is considered vulnerable. Of the nearly 1 million migrants caught crossing illegally last year, U.S. border patrol officials said an estimated 60,000 came from beyond Mexico and Central America.

The price for delivering a Middle Eastern migrant into the United States reached $55,000 this summer, McMahon said.

Colorado is considered a transit point because of its international airport and central location between northern and southern U.S. borders, with convenient east-west connections.

Vans carrying illegal immigrants detained by police in Colorado and other Western states have included "persons from SIA (special interest alien) countries," McMahon said.

"Could we establish that we have organizations interested in the movement of SIAs through Colombia and other countries? I would say yes."

Yet critics question the new priorities.

"Even the most basic functions of immigration enforcement are being abandoned to focus almost exclusively on national security," said Steven Camarota, research director at the Center for Immigration Studies, a research organization that favors stricter immigration law enforcement.

"And targeting enforcement only on people from Muslim countries may lead to a false sense of security because it's very likely Al Qaeda will simply adapt and send terrorists from non-Muslim-majority countries—Philippines, India, Russian Chechnya, China," Camarota said. "We need increased enforcement across the board."

Abuses in civil liberties are resulting, said Ibrahim Hooper, spokesman for the Council on American-Islamic Relations in Washington. He cited a recent Texas case where a Pakistani man was detained for 27 hours in shackles after he returned from a visit to Pakistan via Malaysia.

"If authorities have actual evidence that somebody might be up to no good, they should follow that evidence. But if it is just based on the fact that they are Saudi, Arab or Muslim? That's what we have to watch out for. We have lots of concerns about detention of Muslim- and Arab-Americans based on flimsy evidence or no evidence at all."

American Immigration Lawyers Association spokeswoman Judy Golub said: "We all want to be safer. We need to balance that with the due process and civil liberties that make this country strong. Our government hasn't achieved that balance. If they have good evidence, it would be good to know it."

Homeland Security directors say they are mindful of these concerns.

Concerns about civil liberties "are paramount in my mind," DeMore said. "It's a delicate balancing act between national security and civil liberties. We have not gone overboard."

New Homeland Security agreements with local authorities may help enlist local police in arresting undocumented workers.

Federal enforcers will have to rely to some extent on voluntary compliance from employers, DeMore said. "If you are knowingly hiring illegal aliens, you are hurting America," he said.

Anti-terrorism Plans Stall[3]

By Brad Heath
The Detroit News, April 25, 2003

Key pieces of a high-tech safety network meant to keep terrorists out of the United States are behind schedule, raising concerns that the government hasn't fixed the blind spots in its immigration system following the Sept. 11 terrorist attacks.

Those systems are meant to ensure that the government knows the whereabouts of foreigners studying at U.S. schools and to alert investigators when visitors stay longer than they're supposed to. The government still can't fully do either, a weakness terrorists have exploited in the past to remain in the United States undetected.

The delays—caused mainly by insufficient resources, technological breakdowns and the sheer enormity of tracking millions of U.S. visitors each year—mean shortcomings that helped shelter five of the Sept. 11 hijackers aren't corrected, critics say.

"We can only start sleeping better at night once these things actually start working," said Mark Krikorian, executive director of the Center for Immigration Studies in Washington.

The system designed to track foreign students was supposed to start January 1. But federal auditors say it still isn't ready and won't be fully functional until August. College officials complain that technical glitches have erased student information, among countless other headaches.

Another system that will use fingerprints and swipe cards to track noncitizens when they enter or leave the country is supposed to be turned on in stages over the next three years. But Department of Homeland Security officials already have said they might not meet a 2004 deadline at many of the nation's busiest land crossings, including Detroit.

Experts say both systems are critical. More than a third of the nation's illegal immigrants are people who've overstayed their visas, according to government estimates. That includes four of the 19 Sept. 11 hijackers. A fifth hijacker remained here even though he hadn't complied with the terms of his student visa.

Immigration officials, now part of Homeland Security, say they're working as quickly as they can to get both systems working. They've already fixed some glitches in the student visa system and they expect to be able to track foreigners entering U.S. air and seaports by December.

"We're on target with a lot of this," said Kimberly Weissman, a spokeswoman for the U.S. Bureau of Customs and Border Protection. "But it's fair to say that some of it is still very much in the development stages."

When they work, both systems will identify people who haven't followed the requirements of their visas. Previously, the now-dissolved Immigration and Naturalization Service lost track of so many people officials can't even say with certainty how many are here illegally.

Staffing Shortage

What the government will do when it finds people violating their visas still hasn't been entirely decided. Violations will be reported to criminal databases, for instance, so that local police know that a person's visa has lapsed if they're pulled over. But not everyone who violates their visa will be arrested.

Officials say it will be impossible to track down each person who has stayed in the country illegally.

With only 2,000 investigators to enforce immigration laws, officials say it will be impossible to track down each person who has stayed in the country illegally. "At this point, we're not in a position to be able to go and find that person immediately," Robert Mocny, the head of the entry-exit program, told U.S. Senators last month.

The pace of immigration reforms has frustrated some lawmakers. And they say computers alone won't be able to prevent visa fraud.

"Simply having a database that is operational is not enough," Sen. Diane Feinstein, D-Calif., said earlier this year. "If there is no real effort by the INS to properly manage and analyze data, and follow up when there is evidence of fraud, the tracking system will be no more than a warehouse of useless data."

Immigration officials argue that just having that warehouse is an improvement. And there are already plans in place to deal with visa violators whom investigators suspect could pose a terrorism risk, Bureau of Immigration and Customs Enforcement spokesman Chris Bentley said.

Congress authorized both systems in the 1990s, but they languished for years from a lack of funding until Sept. 11 gave them new life. Together, they represent only a small portion of the broad new homeland security patchwork rushed into place after the terrorist attacks that flattened New York's World Trade Center and damaged the Pentagon with hijacked jetliners.

Behind Schedule

The student visa tracking program, known as the Student and Exchange Visitor Information System, was to be implemented almost four months ago as a way to ensure that foreign students comply with their visas. To do that, the government will monitor in

---

Immigration Changes

- The Student and Exchange Visitor Information System (SEVIS) alerts investigators when foreign students don't comply with U.S. visa requirements. Congress required that it be activated by Jan. 1, but government auditors say it still hasn't been fully implemented. Immigration officials say it's on schedule.
- The Entry-Exit System (EES) tracks noncitizens entering and leaving the country to be sure none stay longer than their visa allows. Officials say they will meet the deadline for airports and seaports this year, but will have trouble meeting the 2004–05 deadlines for border crossings.

---

real time whether students are enrolled in school, whether they have as many courses as their visa requires, and the classes they're taking.

The U.S. Justice Department's Inspector General acknowledged this month that the system isn't yet fully operational. While the tracking database itself was online in time, inspectors say the system can't do its job until it has complete information on each foreign student, something that won't happen until Jan. 1, when colleges finish entering students' names. Until then, only new students will be processed through SEVIS.

Inspectors also said the system has been beset by insufficient staff and technical glitches. Investigations needed to ensure that only legitimate schools used the system were sometimes superficial. And some inspectors responsible for making sure the system works weren't even given the passwords they needed to access it.

"We believe full implementation includes not only technical availability of the system, but also ensuring that sufficient resources are devoted to the foreign student program, ensuring that only bona fide schools are provided access," Inspector General Glenn A. Fine told a House of Representatives panel this month.

Immigration officials disagree. They say they met the Jan. 1 deadline because the database itself was ready on time. And they've met other interim deadlines set by immigration agencies.

"It's unrealistic to say we'd just flip a big switch on Jan. 1 and everything would appear in the system," Immigration and Customs Enforcement spokesman Bentley said. "The fact is, we've rolled out the program, all new foreign students are being put in it and we have real-time access to information about foreign students for the first time. In and of itself, that enhances what we can do for national security."

Yet, colleges complain they're hamstrung by a system that hasn't worked right. At Michigan State University, for instance, staffers have spent entire afternoons entering information about students only to have it lost. And in one case, a student form they tried to print showed up on a printer at a college in Arizona.

"It's been very frustrating," said Peter Briggs, the director of MSU's Office of International Students and Scholars.

Tracking All Foreigners

Far more complicated, officials admit, is a requirement that the government begin tracking all foreigners who enter and leave the country by using biometric identifiers such as fingerprints and photographs. The system is supposed to begin at the nation's airports and seaports by the end of this year. There's a 2004 deadline for turning it on at the nation's 50 busiest land crossings, including the Ambassador Bridge, and a 2005 deadline for every other crossing.

Homeland Security Undersecretary Asa Hutchinson told a Senate panel last month they anticipate having the system up and running at airports and seaports in time. But meeting deadlines for land crossings will be more difficult, he said.

"That means it won't be ready. No way," said Rosemary Jenks, the director of government relations for Numbers USA, a Washington group that advocates a crackdown on illegal immigration.

Immigration officials have acknowledged the difficulties. Some of the biometric technology is new and complex. Environmental rules could slow some of the physical makeovers needed at some border crossings to accommodate new technology. And they need to find a way to make the whole process work quickly enough to keep from creating lines at the border.

"There's no question the land crossings pose a greater challenge," Weissman said.

Critics see bigger problems.

"We'll end up with a decent system eventually because public pressure and national security concerns will make it unavoidable," Jenks said. "But there are going to be a lot of screw-ups along the way."

Report on PATRIOT Act Alleges Rights Violations[4]

NEWSLETTER ON INTELLECTUAL FREEDOM, SEPTEMBER 2003

A report by internal investigators at the Justice Department has identified dozens of recent cases in which department employees have been accused of serious civil rights and civil liberties violations involving enforcement of the sweeping federal antiterrorism law known as the USA PATRIOT Act.

The inspector general's report, which was presented to Congress in July, raised new concern among lawmakers about whether the Justice Department can police itself when its employees are accused of violating the rights of Muslim and Arab immigrants and others swept up in terrorism investigations under the 2001 law.

The report said that in the six-month period that ended on June 15, the inspector general's office had received 34 complaints of civil rights and civil liberties violations by department employees that it considered credible, including accusations that Muslim and Arab immigrants in federal detention centers had been beaten.

The accused workers are employed in several of the agencies that make up the Justice Department, with most of them assigned to the Bureau of Prisons, which oversees federal penitentiaries and detention centers.

The report said that credible accusations were also made against employees of the F.B.I., the Drug Enforcement Administration and the Immigration and Naturalization Service; most of the immigration agency was consolidated earlier this year into the Department of Homeland Security.

A spokeswoman for the Justice Department, Barbara Comstock, said the department "takes its obligations very seriously to protect civil rights and civil liberties, and the small number of credible allegations will be thoroughly investigated." Comstock noted that the department was continuing to review accusations made in a separate report by the inspector general, Glenn A. Fine, that found broader problems in the department's treatment of hundreds of illegal immigrants rounded up after the terrorist attacks of Sept. 11, 2001.

While most of the accusations in the report are still under investigation, the report said a handful had been substantiated, including those against a federal prison doctor who was reprimanded after reportedly telling an inmate during a physical examination that "if I was in charge, I would execute every one of you" because of "the crimes you all did." The report did not otherwise identify the doctor or name the federal detention center where he worked. The doctor, it said, had "allegedly treated other inmates in a cruel and unprofessional manner."

The report said that the inspector general's office was continuing to investigate a separate case in which about twenty inmates at a federal detention center, which was not identified, had accused a corrections officer of abusive behavior, including ordering a Muslim inmate to remove his shirt "so the officer could use it to shine his shoes."

In that case, the report said, the inspector general's office was able to obtain a statement from the officer admitting that he had verbally abused the Muslim inmate and that he had been "less than completely candid" with internal investigators from the Bureau of Prisons. The inspector general's office said it had also obtained a sworn statement from another prison worker confirming the inmates' accusations.

"We have only begun to scratch the surface with respect to the Justice Department's disregard of constitutional rights and civil liberties."—Rep. John Conyers (D-MI)

The report did not directly criticize the Bureau of Prisons for its handling of an earlier internal investigation of the officer, but the report noted that the earlier inquiry had been closed—and the accused officer initially cleared—without anyone interviewing the inmates or the officer.

The report was the second from the inspector general to focus on the way the Justice Department is carrying out the broad new surveillance and detention powers it gained under the PATRIOT Act, which was passed by Congress a month after the September 11 attacks.

In the first report, made public on June 2, Fine, whose job is to act as the department's internal watchdog, found that hundreds of illegal immigrants had been mistreated after they were detained following the attacks. That report found that many inmates languished in unduly harsh conditions for months, and that the department had made little effort to distinguish legitimate terrorist suspects from others picked up in roundups of illegal immigrants.

The first report brought widespread, bipartisan criticism of the Justice Department, which defended its conduct at the time, saying that it "made no apologies for finding every legal way possible to protect the American public from further attacks."

Comstock said the Justice Department had been sensitive to concerns about civil rights and civil liberties after the attacks, and had been aggressive in investigating more that 500 cases of complaints of ethnic "hate crimes" linked to backlash from the attacks.

"We've had 13 federal prosecutions of 18 defendants to date, with a 100 percent conviction rate," she said. "We have a very aggressive effort against post–9/11 discrimination."

"This report shows that we have only begun to scratch the surface with respect to the Justice Department's disregard of constitutional rights and civil liberties," Rep. John Conyers (D-MI) said in a statement. "I commend the inspector general for having the courage and independence to highlight the degree to which the administration's war on terror has misfired and harmed innocent victims with no ties to terror whatsoever."

The report draws no broad conclusions about the extent of abuses by Justice Department employees, although it suggests that the relatively small staff of the inspector general's office has been overwhelmed by accusations of abuse, many filed by Muslim or Arab inmates in federal detention centers. The inspector general said that from December 16 through June 15, his office received 1,073 complaints "suggesting a PATRIOT Act–related" abuse of civil rights or civil liberties.

The report suggested that hundreds of the accusations were easily dismissed as not credible or impossible to prove. But of the remainder, 272 were determined to fall within the inspector general's jurisdiction, with 34 raising "credible PATRIOT Act violations on their face."

In those 34 cases, it said, the accusations "ranged in seriousness from alleged beatings of immigration detainees to B.O.P. correctional officers allegedly verbally abusing inmates."

The report said two of the cases were referred to internal investigators at the Federal Bureau of Investigation because they involved bureau employees. In one case, the report said, the bureau investigated—and determined to be unsubstantiated—a complaint that an F.B.I. agent had "displayed aggressive, hostile and demeaning behavior while administering a pre-employment polygraph examination."

The report said the second case involved accusations from a naturalized citizen of Lebanese descent that the F.B.I. had invaded his home based on false information and wrongly accused him of possessing an AK-47 rifle. That case, it said, is still under investigation by the bureau. Reported in: *New York Times*, July 21.

Boxed Out[5]

By Madhusree Mukerjee
Scientific American, June 26, 2003

After the September 11 attacks, the clampdown on those from overseas wishing to study in the U.S. was inevitable. The PATRIOT Act of 2001 quickly implemented an electronic system for tracking foreign students, and officials are now extensively reviewing visa applications of scientists, engineers and students in technical fields. These and other ongoing efforts are creating a "viscous" visa system, notes William F. Brinkman, president of the American Physical Society (APS). Although such a system makes it harder for would-be terrorists to slip through, Brinkman maintains that it could hobble the U.S. economy and actually compromise national security.

The most visible effect of the visa restrictions may be on the highly international endeavors of physics. At Fermi National Accelerator Laboratory in Batavia, Ill., scientists from Vietnam, China, India and Russia, who all had supplied equipment for one of the detectors, were unable to arrive and operate it. A dozen scientists missed a September 2002 conference at Brookhaven National Laboratory. Vladimir B. Braginsky, a Russian who heads a research group at the California Institute of Technology, could not return in time for a meeting; Rashid A. Sunyaev, another Russian and director of the Max Planck Institute for Astrophysics in Garching, Germany, had to abandon his fall visit to Caltech. Many institutions are advising their foreign scientists to avoid leaving the U.S. (Similar delays are plaguing the biomedical field.)

American colleagues are frustrated that the U.S. Department of State, which in the past was responsive to their concerns, now seems to be turning a deaf ear. Kip S. Thorne of Caltech, who vainly sought updates on the Russian scientists' applications, likens the "visa bureaucracy" to a black hole: "You can't get any information out." The proposed PATRIOT Act II would reportedly classify background material on visas as confidential, which could make it impossible to fix a flawed application.

Senior scholars face delays, but students meet with denials. In 2002 the number of student visas granted was 234,322, down 20 percent from 2001. Stuart Patt, a spokesperson for the State Department, contends that this drop reflects an overall downturn of visa applications since 9/11. At the same time, an APS survey of physics departments learned that 13 percent of foreign students admitted (including 20 percent of those from China) were denied visas, with almost half of those from China facing some kind of difficulty. These problems left science faculty scrambling to fill teaching and research positions and threaten the viability of some small programs.

Part of the reason for the increase in visa denials is that consular officials are being held personally responsible—and possibly criminally liable—if they grant a visa to someone who goes on to commit a terrorist act. Irving A. Lerch of the APS points out that consular officials may not be able to distinguish a benign field of study from a related but dangerous one and would deem it safer to deny visas to most applicants in certain broad categories, such as condensed-matter physics or biotechnology. (In practice, most students are rejected because they cannot prove an intent to return home after they complete their programs.) Even the secretary of state is not empowered to overturn a consular officer's denial of a visa. Yet sadly, the State Department's inspector general discovered in December 2002 that inadequately trained junior officials made most visa decisions and that they were too inconsistent in their background checks to foil a determined terrorist.

What may not make it through is U.S. preeminence in the physical sciences. In science and engineering fields, between 35 to 50 percent of doctoral degrees go to foreigners, many of whom stay: in physics, a third of the faculty is foreign born. U.S. science gathered momentum during World War II, thanks to the influx of trained Europeans. Several estimates attribute fully half the growth in the American economy since then to innovation in science and technology, with "aliens" having played no small part. Lerch fears that a significant, permanent reduction in the numbers of visas for scientists and engineers could cause a long-term downturn in the economy.

In science and engineering fields, between 35 to 50 percent of doctoral degrees go to foreigners, many of whom stay.

Outsiders have also contributed to defense: Albert Einstein and Enrico Fermi, whose ideas lay behind the atom bomb, were originally citizens of then enemy countries. But new regulations prevent foreigners from being employed on a host of "unclassified but sensitive" projects in academia and industry. "There are categories of people who can't work in certain categories of knowledge," notes the CEO of a security-related software firm, who requested anonymity. "There is difficulty getting talented people, across the board." Concern about staff qualifications at the national weapons labs was already running high after the Wen Ho Lee affair at Los Alamos, which promulgated perceptions of racial profiling that made even some U.S. citizens reluctant to apply for positions at the labs. The new restrictions are exacerbating the problem and, according to the trade group Information Technology Association of America, could undermine long-term security.

The most immediate concern, however, is the insensitive implementation of existing regulations. In January the U.S. Immigration and Naturalization Service arrested and detained Pakistani journalist Ejaz Haider for failing to report for fingerprinting. (All men from certain countries must register for background checks.) Haider, who had issued warnings about Islamic holy warriors long before 9/11, was a visiting scholar at the Brookings Institution, a Washington, D.C., think tank, and had apparently been assured by consular officials that he need not register. The affair made headlines in Pakistan. "Everyone here is surprised that the INS is not able to distinguish between friend and foe," comments A. H. Nayyar, a physicist at Quaid-e-Azam University in Pakistan. "This is very scary for friends."

V. Securing Airways and Ports

Editors' Introduction

T his chapter deals with security issues at airports and seaports, hubs of commerce and travel as well as points of entry into the United States. Due to the method by which the attacks were carried out on 9/11, the primary concern was, naturally, airline security. The general consensus is that American passenger planes and airports are probably safer from terrorist attack today than they have ever been before, to the point where many experts believe that a replay of 9/11 is unlikely. Having lost the advantage of surprise, hijackers would now find fellow passengers willing to overpower them, cockpit doors that have been hardened, and pilots who are often armed. The army has also declared itself prepared to shoot down any hijacked plane that does not land immediately (good news, unless you're on the plane). In addition to stepped-up security at airports, however, measures are also being taken at America's seaports to prevent dangerous contraband from landing on U.S. shores. The articles reprinted here examine these new safeguards and suggest others that could still be implemented.

In "Bumps in the Sky," from *Time* magazine, a team of reporters surveys airline security today, pointing out weaknesses, particularly in securing cargo and baggage, but placing them in the context of plausible improvements in what had been an abysmally lax system. A great deal of money has been spent on airline security (sometimes, the reporters say, without sufficient oversight), and more may be needed for projects such as advanced passenger screening or cargo scanning.

Considerably less money has been invested in securing the nation's ports, which present more complex problems and (some experts think) more immediate risks. In "Seeking Safe Harbors," from *U.S. News & World Report*, Pamela Sherrid reviews some of the problems, which affect shippers, manufacturers, and merchants (and, ultimately, the consumer), and can range from identifying foreign seamen to determining the contents of the huge, standardized containers that are packed with goods overseas and then off-loaded from ships onto trucks and railcars at the U.S. port of entry. Determining what is in those containers is a primary concern for security, but transporting the containers quickly is a key issue for manufacturers and retailers, who try to keep warehouse costs low and depend on "just-in-time" shipping. The port of Boston has tried to resolve the problem by introducing industrial-size X-ray scanners, as Abraham McLaughlin relates in "U.S. Port Security: Is X-ray Enough?" from the *Christian Science Monitor*. Boston is one of the few ports in the United States to have achieved a 70 percent scanning rate, but its means of detecting radioactive materials still lack efficiency. However, there are several ways to achieve homeland security goals, and it may not be necessary to do all the checking right in America's own harbors. Increasingly, officials are favoring a cheaper, "layered" approach, where cargo records are inspected at foreign ports, anomalous containers tagged for further investigation at the U.S. port of entry, and stronger seals and global positioning devices used to deter tampering en route.

The smuggling of lethal materials through the ports is not the only danger, however; the ports themselves are tempting targets. Of particular concern to security officials are the poisonous or flammable substances that regularly arrive at seaports and are frequently stored nearby, especially liquified natural gas, a compound so volatile that at present only four ports in the country are equipped to handle it. Those four ports are high on the "watch list" of the U.S. Coast Guard as it assumes its new homeland security duties. The oldest, and for years the least, of American military forces, the Coast Guard has been catapulted onto the front lines of the struggle for homeland security. For a while there was talk of splitting the Guard into two forces, one to concentrate on counterterrorism and the other to carry on with traditional duties—intercepting smugglers, enforcing fisheries laws, and performing search-and-rescue missions. However, in the end the Guard remained intact and was annexed to the Department of Homeland Security, with a greatly enlarged role and a bigger budget. Marilyn Rauber profiles the present-day Coast Guard in "Defending Our Shores and More," from the *Tampa Tribune*.

Bumps in the Sky[1]

BY DAREN FONDA ET AL.
TIME, NOVEMBER 3, 2003

A few days before a college kid named Nathaniel Heatwole got busted for acting like a would-be terrorist, the Transportation Security Administration (TSA) conducted a poll and claims it received good news: most folks believe the agency is doing a decent job. According to the poll, which has not yet been published, about 90% of respondents who had recently flown said security at airports was "somewhat better to much better" than it was before 9/11. It's easy to see why. The federal screeners scanning our bodies, bags and shoes are often infallibly polite, and in their starched white shirts and pressed pants, they appear more savvy than those privately employed workers who could look more bleary-eyed than eagle-eyed. Americans now say they're more hassled by wait times at check-in counters than those at security checkpoints.

Yet in the two years since U.S. aviation began its most radical security overhaul, it doesn't take much to scare us and rekindle this question: Is our system really working? To some experts, the answer is no, and they point to Heatwole's actions as evidence. Saying he was committing civil disobedience to expose flaws in the nation's aviation-security system, Heatwole breached security six times over an eight-month period at Raleigh-Durham International and Baltimore/Washington International airports. He carried aboard contraband such as box cutters and a knife, along with bleach, reddish molding clay (which he hoped would be identified as a plastic explosive) and matches. Frustrated that his efforts were not detected, he finally stowed the items in the lavatories of two Southwest Airlines jets and on Sept. 15 sent federal authorities an email alerting them and identifying himself as the culprit. No one listened. It took a pilot's complaint about a toilet in the rear of a plane for workers to discover the items, which had sat undetected for five weeks.

It's worth pointing out that Heatwole was never a threat. He didn't plant a bomb, and box cutters on a plane aren't a big deal anymore for one simple reason: other passengers. "A terrorist who jumps up with box cutters will probably be beaten to death," says Brian Jenkins, a security expert with the Rand Corp. That said, some security professionals say they're indebted to Heatwole. "That kid is my hero," says Charles Slepian, head of the Foreseeable Risk Analysis Center. "He got us to pay attention to what

---

many of us have known since 9/11—that security at airports is all smoke and mirrors." That may be overstating it, but even Admiral James Loy, the outgoing head of the TSA, admits that Heatwole's stunt "shows us we have much to learn."

First the good news: we're safer today than we were before the feds turned airline security into a matter of national security. Nearly all cockpit doors have been hardened and bulletproofed, and some pilots have qualified to carry guns on board. Crews hold detailed preflight security briefings led by the captain, and, perhaps more importantly, crews are no longer trained to think they can deal with terrorists by themselves. If a threat is detected, a pilot will alert air-traffic controllers, who will likely call in jet fighters while the pilot would land the plane immediately. Some airlines installed video cameras in the cabin and a screen in the cockpit so pilots can monitor passenger behavior. Virtually all large U.S. airlines now have such doors and procedures in place, and many foreign carriers that fly into the U.S. are required to install them as well.

Passengers, their carry-ons and checked luggage are being more rigorously scanned. One thousand bomb-detection machines have been installed in airports since the start of 2002 to search checked

---

The good news: we're safer today than we were before the feds turned airline security into a matter of national security.

---

luggage. The TSA has deployed 5,300 explosive trace–detection devices, which hunt for evidence of bombs and plastic explosives by the residues they leave. The agency is also using bomb-sniffing dogs, hand searches of checked bags and, most controversially, bag matching, in which the airline checks that both passenger and bag make it on board. But that's a requirement for originating flights only, meaning a bomber could hop off during a layover while his bag stays on.

As for those federal airport screeners, they look sharp for good reason. Now on the federal payroll, they're paid more than the minimum wage often earned by their predecessors. Their turnover rate is lower partly because they get government benefits. They undergo more rigorous training and there are more of them—48,000 vs. about 20,000 before 9/11. The TSA boasts that the screeners' efforts have resulted in almost 800 arrests and the interception of 4 million prohibited items. They recently found a gun hidden in a teddy bear and a knife in a sealed soda can, and they eased up on one absurdity: you can once again carry nail clippers on board.

Then there's the invisible security wall in the form of federal air marshals and vigilant citizens. On 9/11 just 33 marshals were patrolling the skies. Today there are several thousand (the exact number, identities and methods are classified). Everyone from passengers to mechanics to airport cops are on the lookout for mischief. The TSA can't take credit for it, but that unofficial screening system is more effective than any piece of technology alone.

All that gives the TSA a measure of credibility in bragging that flying is safer today. Yet no one with a deep understanding of aviation security thinks we're safe enough. Heatwole was hardly the first guy to pull off an outlandish security breach in recent months. In September a New York City man had himself packed in a crate and shipped to Dallas in the cabin of a cargo plane and remained undetected through four airports. In August at New York City's JFK airport, three fishermen whose raft was caught in choppy waters tied it to a pier, walked onto a runway and wandered around for nearly an hour past jets with people on board before stumbling upon the airport's police headquarters. Local airports and law enforcement bear some responsibility for those breaches. But if they are so easy for amateurs and bumblers, how tough would they be for the criminally minded? The TSA is "very much a work in progress," says Gerald Dillingham, director of civil aviation issues for the General Accounting Office (GAO), Congress's investigative wing. Here's where some of that work is needed.

The Achilles' heel of our system is that it focuses more on finding things than on analyzing people or their intent.

Smarter Profiling

Security experts say the Achilles' heel of our system is that it focuses more on finding things than on analyzing people or their intent. Loy, who is leaving the TSA for the No. 2 job at the Department of Homeland Security (DHS), says his "biggest regret was not being able to get a more sophisticated passenger-screening system in place by now." What he's really saying is that we need better profiling. That word butts against our democratic ideal that we should all be treated equally. But the current system—in which information is collected on things like how you pay for a ticket, how often you fly and whether you're traveling one way—can result in Grandpa getting pulled over for the full wand inspection. It's also why up to 20% of passengers on JetBlue, Southwest and AirTran get sidelined, since those carriers sell a lot of one-way fares.

The TSA and airline industry would love a smarter system. "It's the single most effective security measure we could take," says Tom Walsh, deputy head of the Air Line Pilots Association's security committee. But the TSA's proposal isn't winning many fans. That system would assess passengers' risk levels based on a variety of personal data, including criminal records, and give passengers a green, yellow or red light to fly. Get the green, and you would probably breeze through; get yellow, and you and your belongings would be subjected to closer inspection; get red, and you would be subject to extensive questioning and might be prevented from flying. The TSA says the system would automatically delete your personal data a few days after you fly and that the agency would set up a dispute mechanism for passengers who feel unfairly hassled.

Not surprisingly, the idea sends Big Brother chills down the spines of civil-liberties groups and their allies in Congress. It didn't help that a security contractor used itinerary information provided by JetBlue to dig up passengers' Social Security numbers and credit histories. Airlines say they want a system something like what the TSA proposes. But because it's controversial, their strategy is to wait for the government to ram one through and force them to comply.

Training the Air Cops

A few weeks before Loy's departure was announced, the GAO issued two critical reports, one of which said there are "significant weaknesses in the testing and training procedures for TSA airport screeners." The TSA collects too little information on screeners' performance and doesn't yet have a systematic way of training supervisors, the reports found. The inspector general of the DHS discovered that the screeners had been given test answers in order to maximize the pass rate. A classified section of one of the GAO reports suggests that weapons are still making their way past security. And this summer 1,000 screeners were fired because they failed background checks.

Congress is reviewing the TSA's hiring, monitoring and training of screeners, and the agency says it's making changes. A better training program is being put in place for both screeners and supervisors, and all screeners must now be recertified annually. The TSA says it met its self-imposed Sept. 29 deadline for finishing background checks on screeners, whose fingerprints are now on file with the FBI, and it told *Time* that it had to let go of 4% of screeners because they did not pass muster.

The federal air-marshal program has also suffered growing pains. In its rush to get cops in the air, the TSA put hundreds of marshals aboard planes without waiting for them to receive final security approval. Initial training was criticized as quick and dirty. And some marshals seem confused about their role. According to an aviation source, a marshal recently searched an emptied plane during a layover, discovered some pot in a passenger's seat back, and demanded that a local police officer arrest the alleged offender. "Have you ever heard of illegal search and seizure?" the miffed cop asked, refusing to make the arrest. The program is getting an overhaul. The TSA is ceding command this week over the marshals to the Bureau of Immigration and Customs Enforcement. A hiring freeze imposed last year is ending, with plans to replace some of the frequent-flying cops lost through attrition or failure to pass background checks.

The Vulnerable Belly

Security experts shiver when they talk about the nation's cargo-handling procedures. Thousands of low-paid workers have carte blanche to roam airports, ramps and runways without undergoing personal inspections or having their belongings checked. "We put big steel doors on the front of the airport, but the back door is wide open," says Walsh. Cargo on freight planes is rarely inspected. Their cockpit doors, if they exist, aren't required to be reinforced, and security is lax. "There's easy access for a midnight takeover of a major cargo carrier, and a 747 has enough gas on it to make a big impression into the next World Trade Center," says Jay Norelius, security chairman for the Coalition of Airline Pilots Associations.

Despite a congressional mandate that 100% of cargo on passenger planes be screened, it is rarely inspected.

Despite a congressional mandate that 100% of cargo on passenger planes be screened, it is rarely inspected. Cargo companies and airlines have argued that the measure would be too costly, and the government has so far acquiesced. What happens instead is that companies with an established shipping record get a pass under the federal known-shipper program. Yet the program is so secret, no one really knows how effective it is; the number of times a company must ship air freight in order to win trusted status, for instance, is classified. Some airport authorities aren't waiting for the feds to act. Boston's Logan International Airport, where 10 of the 19 hijackers boarded planes on 9/11, just became the nation's first test site for electronic scanning of cargo stowed on passenger flights. The machines use X-ray technology, and if the process proves accurate—and minimally intrusive—the feds will face further pressure to impose such a system nationwide.

Policing the Police

The TSA has been criticized by Congress for approving at least 80 contracts worth $54 million without competitive bidding. In one case, the inspector general of the Department of Transportation found that a contract originally valued at $104 million was allowed to balloon to an estimated $700 million. The agency is nearly $1 billion in the red, and complains about congressional budget cutters, but curious spending practices continue. Many TSA employees cruise around airports in pricey SUVs, not standard-issue Crown Victoria sedans. "Does that make us more secure?" asks one skeptical law-enforcement agent.

The agency is also showing a taste for secrecy. One reason the airline industry has balked at helping the TSA develop a better passenger-profiling system is that the TSA will not share the computer algorithms it's developing to detect threats. "It's a black box," gripes an industry executive. According to critics, the TSA is too inflexible and arrogant. Pilots who have worked with the agency say, "They still don't trust us."

For all these reasons, aviation experts say, there is some merit to gadflies like Heatwole. Says security expert Slepian: "It should not be forgotten that every time he walked up to a screening station, he was subjecting himself to arrest and a possible 10 years in prison." Although he evidently broke the law and faces a criminal charge, Heatwole showed what we have learned to carry since 9/11: a huge personal stake in making sure the system becomes terrorism-proof.

Seeking Safe Harbors[2]

By Pamela Sherrid
U.S. News & World Report, April 28, 2003

If there was any doubt that terrorists could attack the United States via its bustling maritime trade, it should probably have been erased by an arrest in Florida earlier this month. The Coast Guard nabbed a drug dealer for selling phony crew-member papers to leaders of a Philippine terrorist group with ties to Al Qaeda. Those documents, issued by shipping firms, are required of any seaman working on vessels that make stops at ports in the United States.

There's also no question that terrorist acts at U.S. ports could play havoc with the nation's economy. Last fall, the government, the shipping industry, and various importers engaged in a simulation game: What would happen if "dirty bombs," designed to scatter radioactive material, showed up in shipping containers from abroad? The participants found that closing the ports and stepping up the inspection rate of containers threatened manufacturing inventories in a matter of days. This forced, among other dire consequences, an avalanche of earnings warnings that halted trading on the New York Stock Exchange.

Since September 11, the federal government and the maritime industry have made strides in strengthening security on the nation's water borders. The Coast Guard has stepped up patrols, the Bureau of Customs and Border Protection has started targeting for inspection high-risk containers (like those from an unknown shipper) in foreign ports, and domestic ports have tightened up employee identification systems. At the behest of the United States, the 89-year-old international convention governing safety and environmental protection at sea adopted a set of antiterrorism measures. By June's end, the Coast Guard must finalize rules to implement those changes and similar ones mandated by the Maritime Transportation Security Act, which became U.S. law late last year.

But the government has devoted far less money to maritime security than it has to airline security, and many say the challenge is greater. "If you take the paint off the jets of Continental and Delta, their operations are pretty much the same," says Adm. Larry Hereth, the Coast Guard's head of port security. "But waterfronts are tremendously varied and complex, with facilities as different as refineries, passenger ferries, and container docks."

Worries. The industry readily admits that maritime safety is not up to par. "Lots of times there's not even a watch on the gangway," says Stephen White, CEO of consultant Maritime Security Group.

> *The industry readily admits that maritime safety is not up to par.*

The Coast Guard's draft regulations call for measures to prevent hijacking, tampering with cargo, and using a ship as a weapon; for ports to boost security depending on the level of terror alert; and for procedures and drills to respond to security threats and breaches. But even though there's been progress, "many in the industry are just wringing their hands," says Stephen Flynn, a former Coast Guard commander and now a senior fellow at the Council on Foreign Relations.

The stalemate comes not from the rules per se but from the expense of meeting them. Many ports are quasi-governmental agencies that aim to boost a region's employment while operating on slim margins. The Coast Guard estimates that the new safety measures will cost $1.4 billion over the next year, with $6 billion more required over the next 10 years. But so far, Congress has approved less than $400 million in grants to be doled out to the industry, and just $93 million of that has actually been disbursed. An additional $105 million in grants is expected to be announced soon, but there are going to be many disappointed applicants—the total of funding requests for projects equals 10 times the amount up for grabs. The port of Philadelphia, for instance, has a security to-do list totaling $2.6 million, "but we don't have the money," says Bill McLaughlin, head of government affairs for the Philadelphia Regional Port Authority. Many port officials think the feds aren't doing enough. "This is a national defense issue, and we believe the cost should be funded by the federal budget," says Kurt Nagle, president of the American Association of Port Authorities.

If the United States has a hard time getting its own port security shipshape, imagine the difficulties in imposing rules on the shadowy world of foreign-flag ships, which transport almost all the cargo that U.S. ports receive. Congressional Democrats, who were recently rebuffed in their latest attempt to increase federal spending on maritime security, are dismayed that the Coast Guard has handed off responsibility for certifying the security plans of foreign-flag ships to governments such as Liberia and Panama.

"Smart boxes." Money shortfalls may turn out to be less of a problem in the case of technologies that also offer business advantages to importers and exporters. NaviTag Technologies, a Massachusetts-based start-up, for instance, has designed a portable, battery-powered tracking device that fits on the locking bar of a shipping container. The device sends an alert if the container is opened during transit and transmits its position every few hours via satellite to NaviTag. The firm received a government grant last summer to design the prototype. The unit is being tested by big shippers such as Bose, Hasbro, and Hewlett-Packard, which want to keep inventories lean and provide better customer service. "Being able to keep track of assets in shipment would be an incredibly good thing," says Paul Tagliamonte, Bose's director of logistics. NaviTag believes shippers would be willing to pay the $40 a voyage the system is expected to cost per container. As a carrot, U.S. customs has promised that such "smart boxes" will be released more quickly when they arrive in the United States.

But when it comes to the nitty-gritty of port and ship security, like training the thousands of vessel and facility security officers required by the new law, many experts predict the industry will have trouble meeting the July 2004 deadline. As ports compete for limited federal funds, shipping firms are already considering a security surcharge. "Inevitably, shipping costs are going to go up," says John Hyde, head of North American security for Maersk Sealand, the leading container carrier. "A guy who buys one of the 25,000 shirts that was shipped in a container is going to pay more." Just consider it a terrorism tax on the economy.

U.S. Port Security: Is X-ray Enough?[3]

By Abraham McLaughlin
The Christian Science Monitor, May 8, 2003

Down where the city of Boston meets the Atlantic Ocean, where a salty wind swirls amid 30-foot-tall stacks of giant cargo containers, two customs inspectors are doing something few of their colleagues nationwide are able to do: They're scanning roughly 70 percent of the containers that pass through the mid-sized port.

In the cramped control room of a massive mobile X-ray machine, Larry Campbell and Joe Crowley electronically peer into steel boxes, hunting for terrorist weapons among the frozen fish, shoes, shirts, and other cargo.

Every year, 16 million containers move through America's 361 ports. Only 4 percent get scanned—leaving what may be the biggest hole in the nation's terror shield. In a sense, Boston's 70-percent scan rate makes it one of the most secure U.S. ports. It also highlights a fundamental question now circling among port officials, political leaders, and the shipping industry: Would scanning more containers—even up to 100 percent—boost security?

The answer has big implications for the U.S. homeland security effort, global trade, and even retail prices, as scans can add time and money to the shipping process. Yet, even as the debate grows, security experts warn that scanning is only one component of effective seaport security.

"As part of a layered approach, scanners make sense, but the idea that we will scan every container and therefore be confident that everything is hunky-dory—that's pretty much removed from reality," says Stephen Flynn, a former Coast Guard officer who's now a senior fellow at the Council on Foreign Relations in New York. He and others say security requires improvements in intelligence, cooperation with foreign ports, and tracking of containers.

Inside Boston's $2.25 million machine, Messrs. Campbell and Crowley inspect black-and-white images generated as their truck with its X-ray boom slowly rolls past containers. Campbell's three decades of experience are evident when, after just glancing at an image, he declares, "That's frozen fish."

Campbell and Crowley have spent the past 30 years doing mostly low-tech searches—crawling inside containers, randomly poking at contents. So scanning an entire container in just seconds astounds them. "I could retire any day I want," says Campbell, "but I'm staying put because this technology is so amazing."

This X-ray machine is at once revolutionary and insufficient. Increasingly being used at U.S. ports, it was designed to find stolen cars and big drug caches, not briefcase-sized dirty bombs.

Soon, however, the Boston truck will get a radiation sensor.

Yet such sensors are notoriously fickle. The port in Norfolk, Va., tried mounting them on port cranes—with the intent to scan every incoming container. But harsh operating conditions and ever-changing levels of background radiation rendered the devices virtually useless.

One increasingly popular tool is the $120,000 "portal system"—two radiation-detecting panels that containers pass between.

With various technologies proliferating—and with ports seen as one of the weakest security links—the idea of boosting the number of scans is gaining political momentum. A plan by Rep. Jerrold Nadler (D) of New York would require 100 percent scanning. "It's very ambitious, but it's necessary," says Eric Schmeltzer, a Nadler spokesman. "Even if you upped it to 50 percent, there's still a 50 percent chance a boat has a bomb on it."

But others see a more complicated picture. A major upgrade in scanning would detain legions of containers at ports, making them more vulnerable to sabotage or tampering. It would also require thousands of new government inspectors and billions of dollars in salary and equipment costs.

Ultimately, says Dr. Flynn, a more layered approach may be more effective—and cheaper.

For example, the customs bureau's new Container Security Initiative, under which lists of container contents are forwarded to U.S. authorities 24 hours before a shipment leaves a foreign port, gives officials time to assess the risk. They can analyze the contents, the history of the container, and the boat it's traveling on. High-risk cargo is then marked for special scrutiny.

Another key element is securing containers. Most "seals" are now quarter-inch-thick pieces of plastic and metal, and safer seals are being developed.

There's also a growing effort to track shipments with global positioning devices. If a container is diverted—perhaps by terrorists—it would be flagged for inspection.

The global shipping industry can indeed benefit from boosting "supply-chain visibility," Flynn argues. By spending $100 to $150 per container, shippers can get real-time information about the location and security of cargo.

Yet, until big systemic changes actually occur, even skeptics of ramping up scanning admit it may be a necessary option.

Defending Our Shores and More[4]

By Marilyn Rauber
The Tampa Tribune, April 13, 2003

Wartime duty calls the U.S. Coast Guard to missions in distant ports, as well as along our coastlines.

In recent weeks the U.S. Coast Guard gave mouth-to-snout resuscitation to a drowning dog in Texas, airlifted a sick woman from Orlando off a cruise ship and detained two Iraqis on an oil tanker in the Delaware Bay.

In the Persian Gulf, the Coast Guard secured ports, escorted humanitarian supplies to starving Iraqis and captured a few fleeing Iraqi sailors who jumped ship.

Some members of Congress warn that the Coast Guard—whose main assignment these days is keeping America's 95,000 miles of coastline and waterways safe from terrorists—is in over its head.

The lawmakers say the agency is so underfunded and underequipped that the nation's ports are "vulnerable to a catastrophic attack," in the words of Sen. Ernest Hollings, D-S.C. "Do we have more business than we have resources? Yes," the Coast Guard commandant, Adm. Thomas Collins, told a House panel recently. "We have challenges like never before to do all that America wants us to do."

Not only has the Coast Guard yet to arrest any terrorists on home turf—the two Iraqi sailors got the thumbs-up and were allowed to leave with their Qatar tanker—a new report by the General Accounting Office said the war on terrorism is taking a toll on the war on drugs. The GAO, Congress' investigative arm, cited a 60 percent drop in the number of hours the Coast Guard spent on drug interdiction in October through December of last year, compared with the same period in 1998.

In the wake of the September 11 terrorist attacks, the Coast Guard devoted 91,000 resource hours—a measurement used on missions—to coastal security during October, November and December 2001. That number dropped to 37,000 for the same period a year later. That was still a huge increase over the 2,400 hours spent on coastal security in the last three months of 1998.

"Today, a majority of our tasking is on search and rescue and homeland security. We may not be focusing our efforts as much on those [other] missions," said Petty Officer Scott Carr, a Coast Guard spokesman at the Miami-based 7th District headquarters, which covers the Southeast coast and the Caribbean.

4. Editorial by Marilyn Rauber from *The Tampa Tribune* April 13, 2003. Copyright © Media General News Service. Reprinted with permission.

The Coast Guard received a $1 billion budget increase this year and has an active duty force of 39,000, plus more than 4,000 called-up reservists. It insists it can do it all: secure almost 400 ports, pick up illegal immigrants and illegal drugs, stop illegal fish catches, rescue boaters in distress.

Since the nation was put on high "orange" alert March 17, the maritime force has increased its air and sea surveillance by 50 percent—conducting more than 3,000 patrols. Some units have started using bomb-sniffing dogs.

Recreational boaters along the East Coast this summer will find new restrictions on where they can and cannot go. Certain bridges and tunnels will be off-limits, and boaters will have to keep well away from cruise ships and naval vessels.

"If boats are headed for a restricted area or loitering near one, chances are good they're going to be boarded by the Coast Guard," said Senior Chief Petty Officer Tod Lyons, a spokesman for the Coast Guard 5th District regional headquarters in Portsmouth, Va.

"We are beginning to build rings of defense around our ports."— **Secretary Tom Ridge, Department of Homeland Security**

The Senate rejected, along party lines, a Hollings amendment to add another $1 billion to President Bush's war supplemental spending bill to beef up the Coast Guard and tighten port security.

The White House said Bush's $75 billion supplemental budget already includes about $4 billion more for homeland security, including about $2 billion for state and local measures. Bush also announced that starting this summer, the Coast Guard would receive the first of 700 new patrol boats as it gradually replaces its old fleet of 300.

Democrats say the extra money will permit the Coast Guard only to maintain current security levels, not make the improvements mandated in a bill overhauling port security that Bush signed into law late last year. Congress has not approved funding for that law. The Republican chairman of the House panel that oversees the Coast Guard, Rep. Frank LoBiondo of New Jersey, agreed that more money will be needed if the war with Iraq or heightened terror alerts drag on.

Hollings said last month that his state was forced to use parole officers to guard the Port of Charleston because there was no one else to do it. Hollings rebuked homeland security chief Tom Ridge for failing "to get the money out to folks."

Ridge, however, insisted, "We are beginning to build rings of defense around our ports."

The Coast Guard, though, is behind schedule conducting basic port-by-port security assessments. Hollings claims these won't be completed until 2009 under the current pace of funding. Hollings and Sens. Charles Schumer, D-N.Y., and Patty Murray, D-Wash., also warn that terrorists might try to smuggle dirty bombs in sea containers. Of the 6 million containers that arrive in U.S. ports every year, the Bureau of Customs searches only about 2 percent. The GAO, in a hearing last summer in Tampa, warned that many U.S. ports were inherently vulnerable and faced a "formidable" challenge.

The Port of Tampa was cited as typical. The sprawling hodgepodge of public and private facilities is close to downtown and near the U.S. Central Command, which is running the war in Iraq. The port was so busy that as many as 2,000 truck drivers could be found off-loading orange juice alone. On an average day, the Coast Guard reports, it saves 10 lives, answers 192 distress calls, boards 144 vessels, catches 14 illegal immigrants and seizes 30 pounds of cocaine.

VI. Hard and Soft Targets

Editors' Introduction

In some ways, the United States is terrorist's dream—a cornucopia of potential targets that cannot all be guarded at once. This chapter looks at some of the nation's vulnerable infrastructure, in articles that ask the questions, "How vulnerable is this, really?" and "What are we doing to fix it?" *Infrastructure* refers to the essential structures and systems—physical and electronic—that allow our society to function and provide many of the services we normally take for granted. Power plants, factories, electrical grids, rail lines, dams and bridges, schools and hospitals—all are part of infrastructure, and any could be the target of a malicious attack. The articles in this chapter cover some of the areas of concern.

The title of Chris Logan's piece for *CQ Weekly* raises a crucial question: "How Willing Is Private Industry to Identify Its Vulnerabilities and Protect Critical Infrastructure?" The Bush administration assumes "very willing," but the initiatives taken by private industry have been characterized as inadequate by many. However, no company wants to be the first to institute costly security measures while its competitors play cheap and dirty. And no company wants to invest in increased security and then find out that the government wants more, or different, actions. Most of all, no company—no industry, even—wants to look like the bad guy as it passes the costs of security along to its customers. Logan describes the battles in Congress over the security of chemical and nuclear plants, and some early attempts to resolve these standoffs between the administration and its critics. Until they are resolved, security in these areas can move forward only by inches. The special problems of computer networks, which are also privately owned and increasingly interconnected, are addressed in the sidebar "Cyberthreat or Cyberhype?" from the Tech Talk section of *Security Management*.

In "Locking Down on System Security," from *American City & County*, Beth Wade takes a close look at America's water utilities and the people who are working to protect them from contamination or physical attack. Many of the older water systems were not designed with security in mind—indeed, public tours of the local water plant were not uncommon—so there is a great deal to be done. Wade interviews plant managers, security consultants, and employees, all of whom have something to contribute to the picture of an industry in transformation.

Richard Hantula, in a piece reprinted from the 2003 *World Almanac & Book of Facts*, provides a sober account of the prospects for nuclear terrorism. He begins with a survey of the world's stockpiled nuclear weapons, which might be bought or stolen by terrorists, and proceeds to an analysis of nuclear "home cooking," in which radioactive materials—obtained from nuclear waste or even medical equipment—are used to injure, contaminate, and terrify the population at large. Although nuclear weapons are far more dangerous than radiation attacks, the latter seem more likely to Hantula, and he includes instructions on what to do if you are exposed to, for instance, a "dirty bomb."

For sheer terror, little could rival a biological attack. In "Are We Safer?: Public Health" from *U.S. News & World Report*, Amanda Spake surveys the readiness of the nation's hospitals and public health agencies to meet a sudden outbreak of disease. The diseases most feared are highly contagious killers that must be recognized quickly, so that victims can be treated immediately and steps taken to slow or stop the spread of the illness. Although real advances have been made on the diagnostic front, especially after the anthrax mailings of October 2001, in Spake's view the nation's overburdened hospitals are still not equipped to handle the numbers of patients they might receive. Research into vaccines and medicines is going strong, however, as David Malakoff reports in "Big Bucks for Biodefense," from *Science Now*. This brief sidebar illustrates a typically painful dilemma of homeland security. The vaccines and medicines in question, if they could be developed, would safeguard the American people and benefit the entire world, yet the research itself could be extremely dangerous.

How Willing Is Private Industry to Identify Its Vulnerabilities and Protect Critical Infrastructure?[1]

By Chris Logan
CQ Weekly, June 14, 2003

If there is one word that sums up the Bush administration's approach to securing privately owned infrastructure since the Sept. 11 terrorist attacks, it is volunteerism.

The White House has quashed proposed regulations for the chemical industry, opposed legislation to increase security at nuclear plants, and steered clear of imposing new requirements to secure the nation's computer networks. In place of these top-down approaches, the administration has largely relied on the private sector, which owns an estimated 87 percent of the nation's factories, rail lines, power plants and computer networks, to come up with its own strategies to defend against terrorist attacks.

In June 2002, for example, the American Chemistry Council, the trade and lobbying association for the nation's largest chemical manufacturing companies, told its members to study the physical security of their plants and to fix any problems they found. The security enhancements were to be verified by independent third parties, such as firefighters, police officers, insurance auditors or federal or state government officials.

In March, the council announced that its 165 member companies had completed vulnerability studies for their 120 highest priority facilities.

The program is part of the chemistry council's Responsible Care program, described by the organization as "a voluntary program to achieve improvements in environmental, health and safety performance beyond levels required by the U.S. government."

But critics complained the program relied on the good will of the industry, and noted the plan has no requirement that facilities near large population centers stop using chemicals such as chlorine, which could form deadly gas clouds if released accidentally or by terrorist saboteurs. And, critics said, the industry group represents only a small percentage of the nation's chemical infrastructure. Thousands of water and sewer treatment plants, which use chlorine as a purifier, were not covered by the program.

---

1. Article by Chris Logan from *CQ Weekly* June 14, 2003. Copyright © 2003 Congressional Quarterly Inc.

Sen. Jon Corzine, D-N.J., meanwhile, launched his own campaign in late 2001 to impose tough new anti-terrorism security requirements on the U.S. chemical industry.

Legislation that Corzine introduced in the 107th Congress would have required chemical plants to carry out vulnerability assessments, limit the types and quantities of chemicals they keep on hand and, when possible, phase out the use of chlorine and other potentially dangerous chemicals. The bill granted the EPA a lead role in enforcing the new security restrictions.

Corzine's bill also had teeth. Plant operators who failed to comply with the new regulation faced up to a year in prison and fines of $25,000 a day. Repeat offenders faced fines of up to $50,000 a day and prison terms of up to two years.

The bill was approved unanimously by the Senate Environment and Public Works Committee in July 2002.

But after the committee vote, the chemical industry launched an aggressive lobbying campaign against the legislation. It argued that forcing the phase-out of some chemicals would result in costly process changes and strongly opposed the EPA's role, saying the agency had no experience as a security regulator.

Seven committee Republicans eventually opposed the Corzine bill on the floor. It never came up for a vote.

Security for Americans

Meanwhile, the EPA was writing new security rules of its own, using its regulatory authority under the Clean Air Act. But the rules never appeared. Several sources—all of whom favored an expanded EPA role—said last fall that the regulatory approach was scuttled inside the White House.

Corzine reintroduced his legislation early in the 108th Congress, with some changes designed to make it more palatable to the industry—notably granting the new Department of Homeland Security the lead oversight role.

By then, however, the White House was drafting its own bill, which Sen. James M. Inhofe, R-Okla., introduced shortly after Congress returned from its spring break.

The Inhofe bill (S 1043) looks a lot like the American Chemistry Council's industry program. It requires chemical plants to assess their vulnerability to terrorism and to develop plans to fill any holes. And, like Corzine's bill, it includes fines for failure to comply—$50,000 a day for each violation and administrative penalties of up to $250,000.

But as was true of the council-sponsored industry program, Inhofe's legislation sets no minimum security criteria. It includes no requirements for the protection of aboveground chemical storage tanks and says nothing about phasing out the use of chlorine and other dangerous chemicals.

"Unfortunately, the bill does very little to secure Americans who work and live around these facilities," Corzine said in response to the bill's introduction. "The bill may provide an illusion of security, but it's little more than a fig leaf that would leave chemical plants highly vulnerable to terrorism."

Sen. Harry Reid, D-Nev., has met similar hurdles in his efforts to push through stiff new security requirements for the nuclear industry. Legislation Reid sponsored in the 107th Congress would have federalized the private security forces that now guard the nation's nuclear power plants. Reid's bill also would have changed the so-called design basis threat, the number of intruders that guards are required to repel, to include more numerous and more heavily armed attackers.

But the nuclear industry, like the chemical industry, launched an effective campaign to derail Reid's legislation. The Nuclear Energy Institute, the industry's trade association, paid for full-page ads in Washington-area newspapers with large Capitol Hill circulations.

The nuclear industry, like the chemical industry, launched an effective campaign to derail [regulatory] legislation.

The ads featured photographs of well-armed, menacing guards and descriptions of the guards' law enforcement and military backgrounds.

The ads worked. Although Reid's bill passed the Environment and Public Works Committee unanimously in the 107th Congress, it was never brought to the floor for a vote.

Reid, joined by Sens. Hillary Rodham Clinton, D-N.Y., James M. Jeffords, I-Vt., Joseph I. Lieberman, D-Conn., John Edwards, D-N.C., and Tom Harkin, D-Iowa, reintroduced the bill in January. But Inhofe, now the chairman of the Environment and Public Works Committee, had his own legislation ready to roll.

Inhofe's bill would require the Nuclear Regulatory Commission (NRC), to assess the security of nuclear facilities under its authority, as well as the hiring and training standards for plant guards. The legislation also would require more stringent background checks for all individuals who have access to nuclear facilities.

But it would not require the industry itself to bolster security around nuclear facilities.

NRC's Revised Regulations

After the Sept. 11 attacks, the NRC, which oversees the commercial nuclear industry, endured withering criticism from a variety of public interest groups for doing little more than "recommending" that the nuclear industry increase the security around its plants.

The Washington, D.C.-based Project on Government Oversight (POGO) was particularly vocal, accusing NRC of ignoring whistle-blower reports of overworked and lightly armed guards who would be hard-pressed to turn back one or two intruders, never mind an armed team of terrorists intent on stealing nuclear materials or causing a reactor meltdown.

This spring, NRC revised some of its existing regulations, changing the design basis threat to include more armed intruders and increasing the regularity of the force-on-force exercises used to test guards' abilities.

But critics said the new requirements are insufficient.

"The NRC seems to have this backwards. NRC appears to be tailoring its requirements to meet the existing capabilities of the plants' private security forces," said Peter Stockton, a senior investigator with POGO. "Instead, NRC should be determining the realistic threat, then sizing the forces to meet that threat."

Sean Moulton, a policy analyst at OMB Watch, a Washington public interest group, said the administration is relying too heavily on

---

"They're trusting the companies to tell them what's wrong and then trusting them to do something about it."—Sean Moulton, OMB Watch

---

the private sector's willingness to share information about vulnerabilities and to fix its own security problems.

"The administration says this information is critical. If it's so critical, why not require that it be submitted?" Moulton asks. "They're trusting the companies to tell them what's wrong and then trusting them to do something about it."

Apparently stung by the criticism, the Department of Homeland Security proposed a new strategy in April for dealing with the security of privately owned infrastructure. A rule it published April 15 in the Federal Register encourages the private sector to share information about security vulnerabilities, threats or attacks with the government by establishing a system to keep that information out of the public realm.

"The Department recognizes that its receipt of information pertaining to the security of critical infrastructure, much of which is not customarily within the public domain, is best encouraged through the assurance that such information will be utilized for securing the United States and will not be disseminated to the general public," the department said in the proposed rule.

But critics say issuing a blanket disclosure exemption for voluntarily submitted information could keep a lot more than security reports from the public. Companies with poor environmental or worker safety records could keep that information secret by "voluntarily" submitting it to the Homeland Security Department.

"The lack of accountability is staggering," Moulton said. "I'm not even sure Congress will be able to get the full story."

Robert P. Liscouski, the Homeland Security Department's point man for infrastructure protection, conceded that balancing the need to encourage industry to volunteer information with the public's right to know about safety and security issues is a tricky job. "We don't have the answer yet," he said.

Liscouski, a former security executive at the Coca-Cola Co. in Atlanta, sat down with reporters at the department's northwest Washington, D.C., headquarters on June 6 to discuss the department's new cybersecurity division, which will serve as a threat information clearinghouse for public and private computer systems.

The division will monitor threats, help private-sector companies prepare for attacks, coordinate the response to attacks, and provide assistance in recovering from attacks. But Liscouski said the department would not require the owners of the nation's cyber-infrastructure to do anything to bolster network security.

"We don't want to be a regulatory agency," he said. "We don't want to force the private sector to do this."

The best approach, he said, is to give companies as much information as possible and count on the market to force them to do the right thing. Not only will market forces reward companies who protect the physical, personnel and procedural security of their networks, Liscouski argued, they will encourage companies to find ways to assuage consumers' fears about the security of personal data, including credit card numbers and transactions such as bank transfers and online purchases.

Asked whether the department will set standards against which companies would have to perform, Liscouski said no. What it can do, he said, is build awareness within the private sector to existing threats. "We can set expectations for behavior," he said. "The federal government won't solve this problem on its own because everyone owns it."

Cyberthreat or Cyberhype?*

BY PETER PIAZZA
SECURITY MANAGEMENT, MARCH 2003

Is the threat of cyberterrorism a myth, conjured up by product vendors and propelled by the less technically minded members of the media? Or is it a real concern, one that already exists in a simpler form and that is threatening the very infrastructures on which the country is built?

According to a paper from the Center for Strategic & International Studies (CSIS), the answer is somewhere in between. The report, "Assessing the Risks of Cyber Terrorism, Cyber War and Other Cyber Threats," concludes that while network vulnerabilities are a serious business problem, "their threat to national security is overstated."

Critical infrastructures are remarkably resilient, the report states; they routinely fail without creating mass chaos. While "falling trees have caused many electric system disruptions . . . cyber attacks have caused none."

The issue is further muddled by the lack of an agreed-upon meaning of "cyberterrorism." Technology research firm IDC, for example, has predicted that if there is a war with Iraq, it could lead to a major cyberterrorism event. But according to John Gantz, chief research officer at IDC, the firm is talking about an economic disruption (such as a widespread computer virus or denial of service attack against a major online retailer), not the disabling of any part of the nation's critical infrastructure. But the CSIS report even minimizes the impact of these threats, questioning the real cost to the economy of a major cyberevent such as the Love Bug virus and pointing out that, whatever it was, it pales next to the average annual cost of natural disasters in the United States.

While the report acknowledges that nonstate actors such as Al Qaeda might be willing to commit cyberattacks against economic targets, it asserts that the interdependencies of financial markets and the risk of discovery will likely prohibit most nation-states from launching these types of attacks.

William Crowell, former deputy director of the National Security Agency says that the CSIS paper makes a valid point and represents a justifiable backlash against the "sky-is-falling" hyperbole that was rampant last year. While some risk naturally exists, the consequences of cyberattacks are not likely to be lethal, Crowell says, adding that to cause significant problems, an attack would have to continue over a long period of time.

"One of the reasons the 'electronic Pearl Harbor' guys are way over in left field is that they fail to recognize that most of the electronic attacks are not sustainable," Crowell says.

But cyberattacks could still be significant, especially if they are carried out in conjunction with a physical attack, Crowell explains. For example, he worries that terrorists might use computer systems to put out information during a bioterror attack that maliciously steers people toward the event or interrupts the capability of first responders.

Locking Down on System Security[2]

By Beth Wade
American City & County, January 2002

When Milwaukee Water Works began planning for security upgrades in 1999, terrorism was not part of the picture. "We were thinking about vandals and graffiti artists and unhappy current and former employees," says Carrie Lewis, superintendent for the agency. "We thought that the most serious attacker could be a local with a political agenda, somebody like Timothy McVeigh. The international, organized, funded terrorist was not something we thought about."

The Water Works' main treatment plant is situated close to Lake Michigan and abuts soccer fields, beaches and a marina. The city lately has improved public access to the lakefront, increasing visitation to the area—and visibility of the water plant. "Every now and then, a bicyclist would end up on plant grounds, or a soccer player would walk in to see what the place was," Lewis explains. "The fact that those people were getting onto the plant grounds made us realize that we had to tighten up."

By the time Sept. 11, 2001, arrived, Milwaukee Water Works was ahead of the security curve. It had completed a system-wide evaluation and had begun implementing measures to mitigate its risks.

Most public water systems (there are 168,000 in the United States) were not as well positioned as Milwaukee's. As a result, those communities are gearing up for their own security evaluations, which will include indentifying assets, assessing vulnerability and risk, considering countermeasures and weighing costs.

Three Major Concerns

Assessing vulnerability begins with identifying assets (e.g., people, equipment, facilities) and potential threats to those assets. Evaluation must be comprehensive, says Brian Ramaley, director of Newport News (Va.) Waterworks. "[Utilities] have to look at their entire systems, from stem to stern, from the headwaters to the customer's tap, and determine where their systems are most vulnerable," he notes.

Furthermore, the evaluation should focus on activity rather than on the attacker. As Lewis noted, attackers can come in many forms—from employees and vandals to renegades and terrorists—but threats to the water system are limited to what those people can do.

Activities can range from low-level intrusion, such as that described by Lewis, to more serious acts that interrupt operations or even sicken or kill residents. The major threats fall within the realm of physical damage to facilities, cyber attack and system contamination.

Physical damage. Damage or destruction of equipment and facilities, including pumps, pipelines and tanks, can affect any component of a water system, from source and transmission to storage and distribution. How is the intake protected? Where are pipelines exposed? How are tank hatches secured? What is the backup for a facility that is completely destroyed? Those are the types of questions that have to be answered during vulnerability assessments, says Mark Knudson, director of operations and maintenance for the Portland Water Bureau.

Cyber attack. With the advent of supervisory control and data acquisition (SCADA) systems, water utilities have moved steadily from manual to automated operation. What happens if a hacker disables the SCADA system?

"Most water systems in America are able to run in a fully manual mode, although perhaps not as efficiently as we operate with our computer monitoring and control systems," Ramaley says. "Were those systems compromised through some form of cyber attack, there's little doubt that we could continue to function and meet the needs of our customers."

"For most of us, if the system shuts down, we can run it manually," confirms John Sullivan, chief engineer for the Boston Water and Sewer Commission and president of the Association of Metropolitan Water Agencies, based in Washington, D.C. "The real question is: Does anybody know how to do it? When you build a new plant and everything runs by computer, do the operators ever simulate [manual operations]?"

Sullivan also notes that communities with automated security sometimes integrate those systems with the SCADA network. Having both systems on one server presents a two-for-one hit for a hacker.

Contamination. Much of the attention given to water system contamination has focused on system-wide contamination using biological, chemical and radiological agents. However, in October, U.S. Environmental Protection Agency (USEPA) Administrator Christie Whitman stated that contamination with system-wide implications is unfeasible.

"People are worried that a small amount of some chemical or bio-logical agent—a few drops, for instance—could result in significant threats to the health of large numbers of people," she said. "That scenario just can't happen. It would take large amounts of contam-inants to threaten the safety of a city water system."

Vulnerability to contamination still has to be assessed, according to Knudson. "If we look at source water, there might be a concern about contamination that's going to find its way to intake," he notes. "If [the source] is a well field, there are geohydrology issues: What happens if [we discover a contaminant] in one well? Will it show up in another one? In the transmission system, contamina-tion is an issue because there are probably places where you could contaminate an open channel or aqueduct."

Assessing Vulnerability

Vulnerability studies can be performed by utility staff or by a third party, but, ideally, they are done by both. "Outside studies are more likely to pick up things that you would miss in house," Ramaley says. "But you can't just sit back and wait to bring in the experts. You have to look at things yourself and then bring in the outside, fresh eyes to look at your system."

"It really has to be both," Knudson says. "Nobody knows the sys-tem as well as the people who have to make it work. Those are the people that are the operators and the engineers that deal with the system on a day-to-day basis. At the same time, because they deal with it every day, they are [not necessarily objective]. You need the objective opinion of the consultant."

When Milwaukee Water Works conducted its vulnerability assessment, it worked with Sandia National Laboratories, based in Albuquerque, N.M. The laboratory had been hired by the Den-ver-based American Water Works Association Research Founda-tion to study water system vulnerabilities and produce a guide for utilities to conduct their own assessments. It selected Milwaukee as its "guinea pig," Lewis says.

"We were in the right place at the right time," she says. "For two years, we had budgeted money to upgrade security at our facilities. Sandia came [to Milwaukee] in March of this year, and they gave us some specific advice on what they had seen while they were here.

"Some of the recommendations were easy fixes, like making sure that hatch locks are not the kind that bolt cutters can cut," Lewis notes. "Others, like upgrading electronic surveillance and alarm systems, [were more involved]."

Sullivan favors bringing in a third party, too. "I'm not saying it has to be a consultant's paradise, but you need to bring in an out-side consultant to get a fresh pair of eyes. You need a Doubting Thomas," he says. "You need the other person there to ask, 'Why do you leave all your tools for your pump right in front of the pump?' Well, you do that because [the pump has] odd-sized bolts, and the tools are only good for that pump. You're thinking the tools are there to fix the pump, and the consultant is thinking, 'No. Those tools are there to destroy the pump.'"

Nationwide, consulting firms are gearing up to assist with vulnerability assessments. "You've got security experts who know nothing about water and water experts who know nothing or very little about security," Ramaley cautions. "It's really critical that anybody who does this type of work has both sets of expertise and knows how to marry that up so you get useful results."

Determining Risk

Every water system has vulnerabilities, but vulnerability does not equal risk. To determine risk, utilities have to review their vulnerability findings and measure the probability of an attack.

"You have to decide what's important to you and then determine the chances of people getting at it," Sullivan says. He notes that an earthen dam may pose vulnerability, but, if it is not easily accessible, it is not necessarily a risk.

Furthermore, utilities should look at risk in light of potential consequences. "You need to take a look at your system and ask, 'What

---

Every water system has vulnerabilities, but vulnerability does not equal risk.

---

would happen if this went out?'" Sullivan explains. "For example, 'If I lose this pump, what happens?' Maybe the answer is, 'Nothing. I've got another one over on the other side of town, and I'll pump on that one.' But that is where you have to measure your risk."

Having determined their risks, utilities must be prepared to live with some of them, Knudson says. "We're not going to be able to completely eliminate all the risks associated with potential vulnerabilities," he notes. "We just can't afford to do it. We could spend billions of dollars on any given system, and we would still not be there. You have to ask—and here's the key to the whole thing—'What level of risk are we willing to accept?'"

More than anything, that exercise can help utilities focus their countermeasures. "It gives you the information you need to make an informed decision about where you want to spend your money," Knudson explains. "You might decide that it doesn't make sense to put armed guards out at the wellhead because you don't think the wellhead [poses a great risk]. But that becomes a conscious decision in terms of accepting risk."

Delay and Detect

Armed guards? Actually, many of the recommendations for mitigating risk are far more mundane.

"Everyone's facilities were built with doors and gates and windows that lock," Lewis says. "The first thing is to use those things that are already available to us, and the second thing is to get the buy-in of your employees. Those are the people who are at the facilities around the clock, and they can assess whether something they see or hear is unusual and alert others [for response]."

Employees also have to buy in to security procedures, Knudson says. "They have to understand the necessity of keeping doors locked and understand that, if somebody walks up, you don't just let them in."

Public access is a thing of the past, according to Ramaley. Utilities that offered facility tours have, since Sept. 11, locked down. "Many systems have eliminated that," Ramaley notes. "They've shut their gates; they've locked their doors."

In addition to making those changes, water utilities are upgrading security by installing surveillance equipment, and expanding fencing and setbacks, with emphasis on detecting the adversary and delaying him. "I think it's unreasonable to expect every single water utility to upgrade its defenses to successfully defend against organized, armed terrorists," Lewis says. "I think we need to tighten up our facilities so that the casual and lower-level attackers will either go someplace else, or we can delay them long enough to detect them."

Detection is part of the plan in Newport News. There, the Waterworks is considering expansion of electronic surveillance, and it has stepped up watershed patrols. "We serve five jurisdictions, and our facilities touch seven jurisdictions. We've coordinated with local law enforcement in each of those jurisdictions to visit our facilities on a regular basis," Ramaley says. "We've also [contacted] the local FBI office, and I recommend that all water utilities consider doing that. If there is a problem, you're going to have to work with those folks, and it's good to know them ahead of time and have those communication channels open."

Newport News also has worked with chemical suppliers to boost security on deliveries. "Alum deliveries come to us in large tanks. Those trucks are now sealed before they leave the chemical shipping lot, and the seal is not broken until it gets to our site," he says. Similarly, prior to receiving chemicals, Milwaukee Water Works gets the serial number of the tanker and the driver's name from the supplier, and it checks both before accepting delivery.

Although many mitigation measures focus on prevention, others focus on recovery. "Mitigation is sometimes a matter of keeping a spare piece of equipment," Lewis says. "Historically, our inventory was [managed on an as-needed basis]; if you've got eight pumps in a room and one goes out, the other seven will run, so you can wait two months to get parts for the broken one. But now we're operating under the scenario of someone taking out all the pumps, so we will keep the parts that we can in inventory."

Design Implications

In addition to upgrading security in the short term, water utilities are anticipating changes in technology and facility design that could help them mitigate risk. The water industry is pushing for research and development of microtoxicity monitors and gas chromatographs that could help utilities pinpoint contaminants in their systems. Additionally, new plants will be built with security in mind.

> *Although many mitigation measures focus on prevention, others focus on recovery.*

"I think every facility built from now on will be looked at totally different," Sullivan says. "You'll see brick walls, sky lights with bars. You won't just have door alarms; you'll have backup systems—maybe a door and a camera or an infrared [detection device]."

"Security will be incorporated much more completely in terms of alarms and lighting and typical security-type measures," confirms Les Lampe, vice president and director of water resources for Black & Veatch, a Kansas City, Mo.–based consultant. "You're going to see a lot more focus on setback spaces; you're going to see fewer entrances; and you're going to see more control over the roadways, gates, fences and lighting."

Utilities will be looking for optimum safety of source supplies, making them less open and available for contamination, Lampe says. He also expects to see more attention to alternative treatment processes that might provide a higher level of protection than do conventional processes.

"There are a lot of design implications as a result of security concerns," Ramaley says. "We have to look at our facilities as needing to be able to withstand or continue to provide service under potential attack, or at least to know where, if we were attacked, we would be most likely to fail and how we would recover from that quickly. It's not going to be possible to harden all of our facilities so that they can't be attacked, but we can lay our systems out so that recovery can be much quicker."

Quick recovery requires redundancy, and Lampe reports that he is seeing increased emphasis on redundancy, from SCADA backup to power feeds for pump stations. He also notes that physical separation of facilities can assist with recovery. "If you have one pumping facility that is critical to your whole system, [it may be possible] to add smaller pumping stations in different locations, giving you reliability without putting everything in one location," he explains.

A Price to be Paid

From vulnerability and risk assessments to mitigation, shoring up the nation's water systems will be expensive. Where will the money come from?

Congress is debating two bills that could help substantially with payment for assessments and future technology. The first, passed by the House in November, appropriates more than $109 million to assist communities with vulnerability assessments. The second bill, which Sullivan "absolutely expects" to be passed, will fund $60 million for research and development of monitoring technology.

Those sums will not cover security costs for every water system, however. As a result, Sullivan anticipates that cities will share information, with bigger cities assisting smaller ones. "The small guys, who might not have the money for consultants, could work off the big guys," he suggests.

Water utilities may have to raise rates to recoup some of their costs, and they will definitely have to weigh the feasibility of security spending against the capital requirements for infrastructure repairs, adding capacity and complying with regulations.

There is a long road ahead, Ramaley says. "Securing our water systems is going to be a long process," he notes. "It's one that we need to begin immediately, and there is going to be an economic price to be paid. Utilities are going to have to begin down the path and keep moving towards more and more secure facilities."

Nuclear Terrorism: Assessing the Risk[3]

By RICHARD HANTULA
WORLD ALMANAC & BOOK OF FACTS, 2003

The nuclear bomb was used as a weapon for the first and, to date, last time in the bombing of Japan that ended World War II. The bombs dropped on Hiroshima and Nagasaki in Aug. 1945, each the equivalent of some 20,000 tons (20 kilotons) of TNT, destroyed a large part of both cities and killed more than 100,000 people within days. After that, the balance of power in the world and fears of massive retaliation deterred the small body of nuclear nations from using this weapon again.

But the suicide attacks that killed 3,000 people in the U.S. on Sept. 11, 2001, focused attention on a new threat: an apparently well-financed worldwide network of fanatical Islamic terrorists who might not shrink from using radiation as a weapon, perhaps even exploding a nuclear device if they could. Without a definable homeland, such terrorists would not be deterred by fear of massive retaliation—and they probably would not fear the serious health risks from handling nuclear materials.

The Availability of Weapons

Nuclear weapons rank among the most fearsome options potentially available to terrorists. The more powerful devices among today's fission and fusion weapons are many times more destructive than the bombs that hit Japan. Besides their direct damage, they release radiation—which if it does not kill quickly may cause disease and a slow and painful death. However, such weapons are generally kept under tight control. Terrorists would find it difficult to acquire one—though not necessarily impossible; they might steal one, or buy it from corrupt officials, or get it from a nation willing to use terrorism to advance its foreign policy objectives.

According to the Center for Defense Information (CDI), a nonpartisan research group based in Washington, D.C., as of early 2002 the number of nuclear warheads in world stockpiles, including smaller tactical weapons as well as powerful strategic devices, exceeded 20,000. It was believed that Russia and the U.S. each had more than 10,000, China about 400, France 350, Britain 200, Israel perhaps

---

3. Article by Richard Hantula from *World Almanac & Book of Facts 2003*. Copyright © World Almanac. Reprinted with permission.

100–200, India 60 or more, and Pakistan at least 2 dozen. North Korea in Oct. 2002 admitted it had been pursuing a clandestine nuclear arms program.

Concerns over the security of these nuclear devices have been voiced particularly about Pakistan, where Muslim extremists enjoy significant popular support, and Russia, which inherited the bulk of the formidable Soviet arsenal after the Soviet Union's 1991 disintegration but found it difficult to finance strict security procedures. The late Gen. Aleksandr Lebed, who once served as secretary of Russia's Security Council, claimed in 1997 that 84 "suitcase" nuclear devices were found to be missing in the 1990s, though some senior Russian officials have denied this. These small, portable bombs could produce an explosion equivalent to perhaps 1,000 tons of TNT, with a blast radius of 1,600 ft. The Al Qaeda terrorist network has reportedly spent heavily on efforts to acquire portable nuclear devices from the former Soviet Union.

Besides North Korea, Iran and Iraq are suspected of having secret nuclear weapons programs, and may have the necessary materials for making them. If terrorists purchased or stole these ingredients, they might be able to do the same. According to the CDI, some 90 lbs. of enriched uranium and plutonium suitable for weapons have been stolen from nuclear facilities in the former Soviet Union since its 1991 collapse; most of the material was recovered, but not all.

Alternatively, terrorists might opt to build a small, primitive weapon from lower-grade ingredients. According to a 2002 report issued by the Oxford Research Group, a British think tank, terrorists could "relatively easily" make a modest nuclear explosive by obtaining reactor-grade plutonium from MOX, a mixture of plutonium oxide and uranium oxide used for reactor fuel in some countries. According to the report's author, the chemistry involved in separating out the plutonium "is less sophisticated than that required for the illicit preparation of designer drugs." Such a device would be far weaker than the bombs dropped on Japan. But the blast, heat, and radiation even from a bomb equivalent to 100 tons of TNT could wreak havoc, especially in urban areas. The spread of radioactive particles would depend on meteorological conditions and on the height at which the explosion occurred, but the report's author estimated the lethal area for radiation emitted in the first minute after the blast at about 1/2 mile.

Radiation's Havoc in One City

A 1987 incident in Goifinia, Brazil, a city of close to 1 million people at the time, gives an idea of how even unintentional exposure to medical-grade radioactive material can wreak havoc. An abandoned radiation therapy machine containing powdered radioactive cesium-137 was found by scavengers looking for scrap metal. The cesium capsule was cut open, and the "pretty" powder ended up being distributed about the city. Some 250 people experienced significant contamination, over 2 dozen had radiation burns, and 4 eventually died. Over 100,000 were subjected to monitoring. The cleanup operation produced 125,000 drums and 1,470 boxes of contaminated clothing, furniture, dirt, and other materials; about 85 houses were destroyed.

Radiation Terrorism

An easier alternative to obtaining or building a nuclear bomb of some kind is so-called radiation terrorism. In the eyes of many experts this is a more likely path for terrorists. It covers a range of options that fall short of bringing about "mass destruction" but can release enough radiation to induce panic. A piece of highly radioactive material can be transformed into a weapon of terror by merely leaving it in a public place. Terrorists could generate mass fear by hijacking a truck full of radioactive waste and using it to, say, contaminate a public water supply. Or they could seek to release significant amounts of radiation by sabotaging a nuclear power plant or by exploding a so-called radiological, or radiation, dispersal device, or "dirty bomb." This is an ordinary explosive device to which radioactive material (e.g., nuclear reactor wastes or radioactive substances from industrial or medical equipment) has been added. The blast spreads the radioactive particles, which may then be inhaled or ingested, and can remain a lingering source of contamination. While a dirty bomb's toll in death and destruction would probably be small (compared to a true nuclear device), it could create a powerful psychological shock and bring long-term economic and social disruption—the affected area would likely need to be evacuated and decontaminated even if the immediate health risks were judged to be only moderate. Material suitable for radiation terrorism is relatively common. Radioactive waste from nuclear reactors, for example, could be used; it is found around the world and tends to be less well guarded than nuclear weapons. Another potential source is industrial and medical equipment using certain radioactive substances.

An easier alternative to obtaining or building a nuclear bomb of some kind is so-called radiation terrorism.

The first known instance of radiation terrorism occurred in 1995, when rebels from the separatist Russian region of Chechnya buried a dirty bomb in Izmailovo Park in downtown Moscow. The device, reportedly consisting of dynamite plus cesium-137, was not detonated, and was removed by Russian authorities after the Chechens announced its presence. The cesium was believed to have been stolen from an industrial facility in the Urals.

Al Qaeda has reportedly worked on development of a dirty bomb. Abu Zubaydah, who was Al Qaeda's operations chief until captured in Pakistan in Mar. 2002, reportedly told U.S. investigators that the organization had the ability to make a dirty bomb and also get it into the U.S. Officials were skeptical, however.

Radiation and Its Effects

There are various kinds of radiation, harmful or not, whether in the form of electromagnetic waves, like X rays or gamma rays, or in the form of particles, such as in cosmic rays. Light, for example, is a form of electromagnetic radiation that does not, so far as is known, harm living tissue, except in very high doses. A nuclear bomb blast generates a super-sized dose of light, but it also produces ionizing radiation, which can damage living tissue even at lower doses. Such radiation has sufficiently high energy to affect atoms that it hits, causing neutral atoms to gain or lose electrons and thereby become "ions." Ionizing radiation is also produced by the radioactive materials used in terrorism.

Some common forms of ionizing radiation—including alpha particles and, to a lesser extent, beta particles—can generally be readily blocked. Alpha particles are relatively large particles, the nuclei of helium atoms, and travel short distances; they can be stopped by a piece of paper. They ordinarily present a danger only if their source is within the body, as a result, say, of inhalation or ingestion. The much smaller and lighter beta particles, which are electrons, usually won't penetrate more than a few inches into the body and can be blocked by thin layers of metal or plastic. They can cause a type of skin injury that doctors sometimes call a "beta burn," and present a danger inside the body. Other kinds of ionizing radiation—such as high-energy neutrons and gamma rays—have much greater penetrating power.

Highly penetrating neutrons and gamma rays typically make up the radiation released immediately by a nuclear explosion; the relatively large neutrons account for the bulk of the tissue damage wrought. Also associated with a nuclear blast, however, is residual radiation released by the radioactive decay of atoms in the fallout. This longer-term radiation threat is also found in the weapons used in radiation terrorism. Generally speaking, it includes alpha and beta particles, along with, to some degree, neutrons and gamma rays. The precise nature of the radiation emitted, and the length of time the hazard lingers, depends on the radioactive substances involved. Some have a half-life (that is, time needed for half of a given amount of the substance to spontaneously decay) measured in seconds or minutes. Others pose a longer-term danger. The half-life of iodine-131, for example, is 8 days, that of cesium-137 about 30 years.

The damage to cells varies greatly, depending on such factors as the kind of radiation, the dose, and the rate at which the dose is delivered, as well as the cells' sensitivity to the radiation and their ability to recover from radiation-caused injury. The average person experiences in daily life a small amount of "background" ionizing radiation, and many experts believe that exposure to up to 20 times the annual background dose is usually harmless. But exposure to up to 1,000 times the background amount can lead to nausea, vomiting, hair loss, immune system impairment, and blood disease. Generally, if the whole body experiences a rapid, heavy radiation dose, death may follow in hours or days. Less extreme exposure may lead to impairment of organs or body functions, gangrene, birth defects, or cancer.

Countermeasures

Experts point to several ways of reducing the risk of nuclear terrorism. One, of course, is to upgrade the intelligence collected on terrorist groups. Also important is spotting terrorist nuclear devices or materials that are in transit. In the wake of Sept. 11, U.S. authorities began building a network of detectors at key transportation locations, among them airports, seaports, and border crossings. The federal government also stepped up research to improve devices and procedures for detecting nuclear materials, including those whose radiation may be masked by shielding. Sept. 11 also prompted some countries, including the U.S. and U.K., to expand their stocks of the drug potassium iodide, which can help prevent thyroid cancer if taken immediately prior to, or right after, exposure.

Experts point to several ways of reducing the risk of nuclear terrorism.

Also helpful are tighter controls on nuclear weapons, nuclear materials used for other purposes, and nuclear waste. The U.S. government after Sept. 11 pushed for tightened security at private nuclear power plants. However, a September 2002 report by the Project on Government Oversight (POGO), a Washington, D.C.–based watchdog group, found that security forces at many nuclear power plants were inadequately equipped and trained, and suffered from low morale and overwork. A proposed bipartisan Nuclear Security Act would mandate measures to upgrade power plant security such as introducing new hiring and training standards for security staff, assigning a federal security coordinator to each plant, and authorizing plant security officers to use deadly force.

At the G8 summit of major powers in June 2002, Western leaders agreed to contribute $20 billion over the next decade, including $10 billion from the U.S., to projects aimed at countering "the spread of weapons and materials of mass destruction." Nuclear weapons and materials in Russia were a major focus of this initative, which included "dismantlement of decommissioned nuclear submarines, the disposition of fissile materials, and the employment of former weapons scientists" (this last point reflected concern that highly skilled but now jobless engineers and scientists might accept work from terrorists). Outside Russia, highly enriched uranium can be found at well over 300 research reactors in nearly 60 countries, in some cases under very lax security.

In Aug. 2002 hundreds of Yugoslav scientists, technicians, and officials, with the aid of U.S., Russian, and International Atomic Energy Agency (IAEA) specialists and under the watchful protection of Yugoslav Army helicopters and troops, removed nearly 100 lbs. of weapons-grade uranium—enough for 2 or 3 bombs—from a decrepit research institute in Belgrade. This was the first of what many hoped would be a series of multinational operations to secure such materials.

A June 2002 report by the IAEA noted that security problems extend far beyond the relatively few facilities with plutonium or enriched uranium. Many governmental, educational, and industrial facilities around the world have other radioactive materials that could be used in a dirty bomb. According to the report, over 100 countries lack adequate controls to prevent, or detect the theft of, these materials. Since 1996, U.S. companies have lost track of some 1,500 radioactive sources according to the U.S. Nuclear Regulatory Commission. Contentious talks under UN auspices have been under way since the late 1990s on an international Draft Convention on Nuclear Terrorism. Such a pact, if agreed upon, could help standardize and streamline procedures for suppressing nuclear terrorism.

What to Do in a Radiation Emergency

In the event of a radiation emergency, the U.S. Centers for Disease Control and Prevention (CDC) recommends that you find shelter in a stable building and check your radio or TV for emergency-alert information. If you live near a nuclear power plant, you should have a copy of its emergency plan, available from the plant. Every household should also have its own emergency plan.

Officials may advise you to "shelter in place," in which case you should avoid opening doors and windows, close fireplace dampers, and turn off fans, air conditioners, and heating units that draw in outside air; it's generally safer in an inner room or basement. If possible, change your clothes, sealing the potentially contaminated clothes in a plastic bag. Showering or washing yourself will reduce any radioactive particles on the skin. It's a good idea to always keep an emergency kit on hand, with items such as flashlight, portable radio, extra batteries, bottled water, canned and packaged food, hand-operated can opener, first-aid kit, and needed prescription drugs and personal items. If told to evacuate to another location, it is useful to bring such items, plus cash and credit cards. You may have to leave pets behind, since they are often not allowed in emergency shelters.

Are We Safer?: Public Health[4]

By Amanda Spake
U.S. News & World Report, September 15, 2003

Jerome Hauer had been urging federal officials to take bioterrorism seriously ever since he completed New York City's first comprehensive terrorism response plan in 2000. As director of the city's Office of Emergency Management and then later as a consultant, Hauer—like many experts—knew that government agencies lacked the basic lab facilities, computers, personnel, and training needed to respond to terrorist attacks. Two days after the planes hit the World Trade Center towers, Secretary of Health and Human Services Tommy Thompson arrived in New York to offer the city's Office of Emergency Management more help—and to ask Hauer for his. Thompson, like Hauer and others, feared a bioterrorist attack could be next.

Hauer is now HHS's assistant secretary for public-health emergency preparedness planning—in effect, the nation's first public-health preparedness czar—and a lot has changed. More than $6.6 billion in federal funds has been spent on biopreparedness and rebuilding the nation's public-health system, and an additional $3.6 billion has been requested for 2004. "The public-health system is better prepared to deal with an emergency . . . than it was two years ago," says Patrick Libbey, executive director of the National Association of County and City Health Officials. "But there is still a ways to go."

Before the 19 terrorists converted their four hijacked planes into deadly missiles, bioterrorism funding had been directed largely to programs within the Department of Defense, where, says Hauer, "the focus was on buying toys, not systems." DOD, for example, bought 3.3 million biological and chemical protective suits, but their long-term effectiveness is unknown, because DOD has lost the purchase records showing the expiration dates. When a Florida newspaper employee died of inhalation anthrax in October 2001, and then 22 others contracted the disease, it became clear that a biological attack was no longer theoretical. HHS "stumbled a bit" in responding, concedes Hauer. Information was not available or not consistent, and federal scientists misunderstood the efficiency with which mail sorters could aerosolize the spores—resulting in five deaths. Yet, inhalation anthrax proved fatal in just half of the cases, in part, because a new, multiple-antibiotic treatment was pioneered during the attacks. A new anthrax vaccine is also nearing clinical trials and should be available by September 2004.

The Topoff II exercise in May 2003, which plotted response to a fictional "dirty bomb" in Seattle and the release of plague in Chicago, revealed that major gaps still exist in hospitals' ability to cope with hundreds of patients at once. Half of hospitals, for example, have fewer than six ventilators per 100 beds, yet one per patient would be needed to treat inhalation anthrax or botulism. Four out of five hospitals now have a bioterrorism response plan, but fewer than half have tested them.

The smallpox vaccination program, announced by President Bush in December 2002, aimed to protect some 500,000 military personnel and 500,000 civilian healthcare workers. Eradicated as a natural disease in 1980, the virus that causes smallpox still exists—officially at least—only in labs in the United States and Russia.

But the new smallpox vaccination effort has brought some troubling surprises. Of the 38,000 healthcare workers vaccinated so far, 21 suffered heart inflammation, and eight experienced other cardiac problems, including five heart attacks, two fatal. As a result, the civilian smallpox vaccination program, estimated to cost about $100 million through this year, has come to a virtual halt. Vaccination is now being viewed only as one part of smallpox preparedness. And a new study indicates those vaccinated even 75 years ago retain some immunity to smallpox, perhaps reducing the need for—and risk of—revaccination.

Big Bucks for Biodefense*

BY DAVID MALAKOFF
SCIENCE NOW, SEPTEMBER 8, 2003

The biodefense bandwagon is rolling. The U.S. government has awarded eight lead institutions grants totaling $350 million over the next 5 years to establish collaborative research centers that will focus on everything from understanding potential bioterror agents to developing new vaccines.

"These grants are a big step," says Eli Lilly executive Gail Cassel, head of the American Society for Microbiology's public affairs board. "They will help build the research community we need to develop [biodefenses] . . . and respond to infectious diseases."

The awards, announced on 4 September by Department of Health and Human Services Secretary Tommy Thompson, are among the government's biggest research-related responses so far to the 2001 anthrax letter attacks. After the attacks, the White House requested billions of dollars to shore up bioterror preparedness. Blue-ribbon advisory panels recommended that the government set up 10 regional centers of excellence to speed the development of therapies, vaccines, and diagnostics. Last year, the National Institute of Allergy and Infectious Diseases (NIAID) opened a fast-track competition to host the first centers, and universities scrambled to assemble consortia to compete for the funds (*Science*, 6 September 2002, p. 1630).

The eight winning teams bring diverse talents to the task, from basic research prowess to vast experience validating vaccines, says NIAID Director Anthony Fauci. Each will focus its $35 million to $50 million 5-year budget on a few priorities. For instance, a consortium of six southeastern schools, led by immunologist Barton Haynes of Duke University in Durham, North Carolina, will concentrate on anthrax, plague, and orthopoxviruses such as smallpox and monkeypox. The midwestern center, led by microbiologist Olaf Schneewind of the University of Chicago, has botulism, tularemia, and hemorrhagic fever viruses on the to-do list for its 14 members.

Later this month, NIAID expects to announce two biosafety level 4 laboratories.

Bibliography

Books

Brill, Steven. *After: How America Confronted the September 12 Era*. New York: Simon & Schuster, 2003.

Brown, Cynthia, ed. *Lost Liberties: Ashcroft and the Assault on Personal Freedom*. New York: New Press, 2003.

Campbell, Kurt M., and Michele A. Flournoy. *To Prevail: An American Strategy for the Campaign Against Terrorism*. Washington, D.C.: Center for Strategic and International Studies, 2001.

Cole, David. *Enemy Aliens: Immigrants' Rights and American Freedoms in the War on Terrorism*. New York: New Press, 2003.

Condon, Bradly J., and Tapen Sinha. *Drawing Lines in Sand and Snow: Border Security and North American Economic Integration*. Armonk, NY: M. E. Sharpe, 2003.

Cordesman, Anthony H. *Terrorism, Asymmetric Warfare, and Weapons of Mass Destruction*. New York: Praeger, 2001.

Dempsey, James X., and David Cole. *Terrorism and the Constitution: Sacrificing Civil Liberties in the Name of National Security*. New York: New Press, 2002.

Frist, William H. *When Every Moment Counts: What You Need to Know about Bioterrorism from the Senate's Only Doctor*. Lanham, MD: Rowman & Littlefield, 2002.

Gertz, Bill. *Breakdown: How America's Intelligence Failures Led to September 11*. Washington, D.C.: Regnery Pub., 2002.

Goldberg, Danny, Victor Goldberg, and Robert Greenwald, eds. *It's a Free Country: Personal Freedom in America after September 11*. New York: Nation Books/Thunder's Mouth Press, 2003.

Gottfried, Ted. *Homeland Security Versus Constitutional Rights*. Brookfield, CT: 21st Century Books, 2003.

Hutton, Donald B. *Guide to Homeland Security Careers*. Hauppauge, NY: Barrons, 2003.

Larson, Eric V. *Preparing the U.S. Army for Homeland Security: Concepts, Issues, and Options*. Santa Monica, CA: Rand, 2001.

Leone, Richard C., and Greg Anrig, Jr., eds. *The War on Our Freedoms: Civil Liberties in an Age of Terrorism*. New York: BBS Public Affairs, 2003.

Malkin, Michelle. *Invasion: How America Still Welcomes Terrorists, Criminals, and Other Foreign Menaces to Our Shores*. Washington, D.C.: Regnery Pub., 2002.

Miller, John, Michael Stone, and Chris Mitchell. *The Cell: Inside the 9/11 Plot and Why the CIA and FBI Failed to Stop It*. New York: Hyperion, 2002.

Nestle, Marion. *Safe Food: Bacteria, Biotechnology, and Bioterrorism*. Berkeley, CA: University of California Press, 2003.

Posner, Gerald L. *Why America Slept: The Failure to Prevent 9/11*. New York: Random House, 2003.

Preston, Richard. *The Hot Zone*. New York: Random House, 1994.

Ranum, Marcus J. *Myth of Homeland Security*. Indianapolis, IN: Wiley Publishing, 2003.

Safir, Howard. *Security: Policing Your Homeland, Your City, Yourself*. New York: Thomas Dunne Books, 2003.

Schneier, Bruce. *Beyond Fear: Thinking Sensibly About Security in an Uncertain World*. New York: Copernicus Books, 2003.

Schulhofer, Stephen J. *The Enemy Within: Intelligence Gathering, Law Enforcement, and Civil Liberties in the Wake of September 11*. New York: Century Foundation, 2002.

Schweitzer, Yoram, and Shaul Shai. *An Expected Surprise—The September 11th Attacks in the USA and Their Ramifications*. Herzliya, Israel: Mifalot, IDC & ICT Publications, 2002.

Vanden Heuvel, Katrina, ed. *A Just Response: The* Nation *on Terrorism, Democracy, and September 11, 2001*. New York: Thunder's Mouth Press/ Nation Books, 2002.

Wells, Donna Koren, and Bruce C. Morris. *Live Aware, Not in Fear: The 411 after 9-11: A Book for Teens*. Deerfield Beach, FL: Health Communications, 2002.

Web Sites

This section offers the reader a list of Web sites that can provide more extensive information on issues related to homeland security. These Web sites also include links to other sites that may be of help or interest. Due to the nature of the Internet, we cannot guarantee the continued existence of a site, but at the time of this book's publication, all of these Internet addresses were operational.

American Red Cross—Homeland Security Advisory System

www.redcross.org / services / disaster / beprepared.hsas.html

The American Red Cross has set up this Web site to explain the different threat levels devised by the Department of Homeland Security and to provide guidelines and recommendations for dealing with various kinds of emergencies, from terrorist attacks to blackouts.

ANSER Institute for Homeland Security

www.homelanddefense.org

Begun in California in 1958, the ANSER Institute, whose home office is in Arlington, Virginia, is a nonprofit organization that strives to lead the debate for national security through executive-level education, public awareness programs, workshops for policy makers, and online publications.

The Liberty Dogs

www.thelibertydogs.com

The Liberty Dogs, a nonpartisan watch group with members from a variety of political parties, monitors the activities and plans of the Department of Homeland Security. The Web site includes news bulletins and links to information about the latest homeland security developments and provides an arena for expressing concerns about what its members perceive as excessive restrictions placed on civil liberties by the U.S. government.

National Homeland Security Knowledgebase

www.twotigersonline.com / resources.html

Run by Two Tigers Radiological, a supplier of equipment needed in the event of a nuclear or radiation emergency, this Web site provides links to information about homeland security, as well as methods for coping with a variety of emergencies, including nuclear/radiological, biological, and chemical, as well as explosives and other hazardous devices, and natural disasters.

Transportation Security Administration (TSA)

www.tsa.gov / public

This is the official Web site of the Transportation Security Administration, which strives to protect the nation's transportation systems so that all Americans may enjoy freedom of movement and commerce. The site provides travel tips, transportation news and events, and information about the latest federal regulations affecting travel and shipping.

USA PATRIOT Act—Electronic Privacy Information Center (EPIC)
www.epic.org / privacy / terrorism / hr3162.html

This site contains the full text of the USA PATRIOT Act, passed on October 24, 2001. EPIC, founded in Washington, D.C., in 1994, attempts to bring civil liberties issues to the public's attention and champions individuals' privacy, the First Amendment, and the principles of the U.S. Constitution.

U.S. Border Patrol
USCIS.gov / graphics / shared / lawenfor / bpatrol

The Border Patrol is a uniformed law enforcement service that guards U.S. borders to prevent smuggling and illegal entry and participates in rescue operations.

U.S. Bureau of Immigration and Customs Enforcement
www.bice.immigration.gov

This agency combines the law enforcement functions of the old Immigration and Naturalization Service and the duties of the Customs Bureau. It works to prevent drugs, weapons, money, and human beings from being smuggled across U.S. borders; tracks down violators, including illegal aliens, inside the United States; and pursues cases of immigration fraud.

U.S. Coast Guard
www.USCG.mil

The Coast Guard protects U.S. ports, enforces shipping laws, pursues suspicious craft, and performs search and rescue missions at sea. This Web site describes its history and mission, as well as details of recent activities.

U.S. Department of Homeland Security
www.homelandsecurity.org.

The department's official Web site includes connections to the *Journal of Homeland Security* (a refereed, scholarly publication) and the department's newsletter, as well as the many agencies under the department's purview.

Water Information Sharing and Analysis Center
www.waterisac.org.

This Web site focuses on the protection of water and wastewater facilities from contamination, physical attack, and cyber attack. WaterISAC employs analysts and provides access to other sites so that information can be evaluated and shared among facilities, and incidents reported quickly.

Additional Periodical Articles with Abstracts

More information dealing with homeland security and related subjects can be found in the following articles. Readers who require a more comprehensive selection are advised to consult *Readers' Guide to Periodical Literature*, *Readers' Guide Abstracts*, *Social Sciences Abstracts*, and other Wilson publications.

The Mother of Reinvention (Why Americans Don't Want a National ID Card). Walter Kirn. *Atlantic Monthly,* v. 289 pp28–29 May 2002.

Hostility toward proposals for a new national identity card, Kirn suggests, might be accounted for by the fact that Americans have always reserved the right to reinvent and improve themselves. In America, to be sorted, tagged, and permanently filed is to lose a part of one's soul. In principle, Kirn asserts, unless and until a citizen asks the state for something in return, his identity or lack thereof is purely his own business. Most Americans no longer cringe at the prospect of being reduced to numbers, but the national ID cards being proposed would take the process to a whole new level by serving as high-tech surrogate selves. However troubling the prospects of being tracked, hacked, or harassed through a national ID system, the author believes that the true danger is the effect such a system might have on Americans' own definition of American identity.

Northern Command Adds Teeth to Homeland Defense, Security. William B. Scott. *Aviation Week & Space Technology*, v. 157 pp29–30 October 7, 2002.

Scott explains that the recent activation of the U.S. Northern Command (NORTHCOM) was the first time since George Washington's era that a single military commander has been charged with protecting the homeland. The unit's establishment under the Pentagon's 2002 Unified Command Plan was motivated by the September 11 terrorist attacks, which highlighted Defense Department and government interagency defense and security. The goal of NORTHCOM is to deter, prevent, and defeat threats and aggression aimed at the United States, its territories, and interests. In addition, under its charter, the unit can offer military aid to civil authorities when approved by the president or the secretary of defense. NORTHCOM's first commander is General Ed Eberhart, who wants to preempt another terrorist strike rather than deal with the aftermath of one, and its area of responsibility includes all air, land, and sea approaches to North America.

Rights, Liberties, and Security: Civil Rights and National Security in Post–9/11 America. Stuart Taylor, Jr. *Brookings Review,* v. 21 pp25–31 Winter 2003.

The author argues that the urgency of infiltrating clandestine terrorist cells makes it essential that Congress undertake a candid and systematic reassessment of the civil liberties laws that hinder the government's core investigative and detention powers. America is being confronted by dangers without precedent: a mass movement of militant Islamic terrorists who are determined to kill as many people as possible. Ultimately, according to Taylor, the number of casualties can be kept at a minimum only by imprisoning or killing as many as possible of the hundreds or thousands of potential Al Qaeda terrorists whose plan is to infiltrate American society and avoid attention until they attack. In the author's view, serious national debate and deliberate congressional action should supplant what has so far been essentially ad hoc presidential improvisation.

Pandora's Cargo Boxes (Protecting U.S. Ports). Adam Aston. *Business Week*, pp47–48 October 22, 2001.

Aston identifies America's seaports as a gaping hole in national security. As the United States races to secure itself against terrorism, airport security has come under intense scrutiny. Nonetheless, the easiest way for terrorists to transport lethal chemicals, bio weapons, or even homemade nuclear devices to Los Angeles, New York, Miami, or Chicago would be via container. Packed with $1.1 trillion worth of imported goods, the 18.5 million containers that arrive in the United States each year by truck, railcar, and ship constitute a vital economic lifeline and the most vulnerable link in the nation's transportation infrastructure. Besides being gateways to all the major cities, Aston reports, each port is also a tempting target in its own right.

Transportation: Loading Up on New Rules. Esther D'Amico. *Chemical Week,* v. 165 pp16+ January 15, 2003.

D'Amico discusses the new rules issued by the Department of Homeland Security governing the transportation and storage of chemicals and hazardous materials.

Is Homeland Security Keeping America Safe? Jeff Stein. *CQ Weekly*, v. 61 pp1476–7 June 14, 2003.

The author assesses the progress of the new Department of Homeland Security. He sees real improvement in its handling of immigration controls but points out that intelligence services are still uncoordinated and largely outside the department's authority. Other problems include bureaucratic infighting; the opposition of powerful interests, such as the chemical industry; and hostile reactions to the PATRIOT Act, which more than 100 communities have resolved not to recognize.

Security Blanket. Chana R. Schoenberger. *Forbes,* v. 171 pp54–55 April 14, 2003.

In the author's opinion, it is extremely difficult to prevent terrorists from smuggling weapons through U.S. ports. Only two percent of the six million cargo containers that land in the United States each year are physically searched. To reduce the threat, Customs is putting inspectors in 18 of the 20 biggest foreign ports and ordering shippers to provide considerably more detailed manifests one week earlier than before. In addition, Schoenberger reports, the Department of Homeland Security recently hired 270 additional Customs inspectors, who will be given high-tech equipment valued at $45 million to scan for explosives, nuclear weapons, and biological and chemical agents within closed containers.

Regime Change. Lewis H. Lapham. *Harper's*, v. 306 pp34+ February 2003.

Lapham, editor of *Harper's*, castigates the Bush administration for ignoring civil liberties, and the American people for tamely acquiescing in the misuse of government power.

Business Blacklists. Michael Scherer. *Mother Jones*, v. 28 pp17–18 May/June 2003.

Scherer reports that profiling of consumers has become more common since September 11, 2001, as the federal government increasingly requires private enterprise to do the work of law enforcement. Two weeks after the terrorist attacks, President Bush issued an executive order extending sanctions already applied to banks to all businesses, and the administration started to add the names of hundreds of suspected terrorists to the U.S. Treasury's Office of Foreign Asset Control (OFAC) list. In addition, the USA PATRIOT Act of October 2001 requires financial institutions to check every new customer against OFAC's online database, which currently contains 10,000 names and aliases, and federal officials are drafting rules that would mandate customer screening at casinos, insurance companies, car dealerships, travel agencies, pawnbrokers, and gem dealers. In 2002, businesses requested that the Treasury office investigate over 45,000 customers. The writer discusses the negative effect of the OFAC list on innocent Americans with names used by suspected terrorists.

Worlds Apart. Siobhan Gorman. *National Journal*, v. 35 pp2485+ August 2, 2003.

Using an analogy drawn from the best-seller *Men Are from Mars, Women Are from Venus,* Gorman contrasts the institutional cultures of the FBI and the CIA. FBI agents focus on solving crimes and winning cases, in a clear-cut manner; CIA agents, on predicting crimes and thwarting their commission, often in a climate of uncertainty. The FBI, operating within the United States, is more scrupulous about legality, Gorman says; its agents concentrate on particular assignments and rarely develop long-term relations with pet informants. The CIA, operating outside the United States, feels less constrained by laws; it encourages speculative thinking and the cultivation of sources over time. The author describes several pilot attempts to bring the agencies together and make each more familiar with the other's way of operating.

At First Glance. John Derbyshire. *National Review*, v. 53 pp42–44 October 5, 2001.

Derbyshire argues that racial profiling is a practical and perfectly sensible tool for preventing crime and terrorism. Since the terrorists struck, civil libertarians are warning that, in the present climate of crisis and national danger, ancient liberties could be sacrificed to the general desire for greater security. Derbyshire says America can and should impose a system of "racial profiling" where it matters most, however, especially in airport security. When boarding a plane, documents need to be presented, names declared, and words exchanged, so despite the problem that "of Middle Eastern appearance" is possibly a more dubious description even than "black" or "Hispanic," security officials have a much richer supply of data than a mere visual check. There should be profiling at airports, Derbyshire insists, because, though not infallible, it is a useful aid in identifying those who want to harm Americans.

Security Is Looser on Corporate Aircraft. Joe Sharkey. *New York Times*, pC7 October 28, 2003.

Sharkey reports that many of the nation's corporately owned aircraft, ranging from two-seaters to passenger jets, regularly take off without the security measures that are now required on commercial flights. Security policies for these aircraft are established by the corporations themselves or by the companies that lease the planes; some are more careful than others. It is no longer the case, he says, that most of the passengers on a corporate flight know and can vouch for each other.

Fortress America. Matthew Brzezinski. *New York Times Magazine,* pp38+ February 23, 2003.

Establishing genuine homeland security would cost many trillions of dollars and completely alter the way Americans go about their lives, Brzezinski writes. In preparing for a war against Iraq, Americans have begun to realize that this could be a war on two fronts, one in the Middle East and the other on home ground. For the first time in history it appears plausible that an enemy could mount a sustained attack on the United States by using weapons of terrorism to strike, among other things, such "soft" targets as offices, shopping malls, restaurants, and hotels. The writer discusses how the American way of life would be changed, and American morale altered, if certain proposals for combating terrorism were implemented.

Ridge Against the Machine. Steven Brill. *Newsweek*, v. 139 pp32–36 March 18, 2002.

According to Brill, Tom Ridge and his Office of Homeland Security are quietly making things happen on Capitol Hill. Ridge has organized 22 multiagency groups—on subjects ranging from biopreparedness to food security to irradiation awareness—that have been quietly working through the old Executive

Office Building. Although much of the work is not visible yet and they are working against a system full of people unused to quick change, the groups, Brill says, do seem to be getting things done, primarily by attacking the bureaucracy that would oppose them, turning ideas, funding, and operating control over to the agency best suited to take the lead in a given area.

A Watchful Eye. Steven Brill. *Newsweek*, v. 141 pp32–33 February 24, 2003.

The debate over homeland security is set to become increasingly partisan as the 2004 elections approach. The writer attempts to separate the rhetoric from the reality.

How Much Safer Are We? Michael Hirsh. *Newsweek*, v. 142 p46 September 15, 2003.

Despite progress since the terrorist attacks of September 11, 2001, Hirsh says, the United States remains vulnerable to attack. Intelligence about terrorism threats appears to be as sketchy as it was before the World Trade Center attacks. Tom Ridge, the head of Homeland Security, argues that some success so far can be measured in the quiet since the terror and anthrax attacks of almost two years ago, but Ridge admits that the intelligence he receives is simply not good enough to alert a particular city or region to a specific threat. Already billions in debt from funding overtime and new equipment, cities are now rebelling against Washington's demands to deploy more police and emergency officials during high terror alerts, Hirsh reports.

Nuclear Power Plants and Their Fuel as Terrorist Targets. Douglas M. Chapin and Karl P. Cohen. *Science*, v. 297 pp1997–8 September 20, 2002.

The authors say that much misinformation is circulating about the vulnerability of nuclear shipments and power plants to terrorist attack. Recent media reports and public statements have alleged that spent nuclear fuel casks being shipped to Nevada are liable to terrorist attacks that could lead to a major catastrophe. However, extensive analysis, supported by full-scale field tests, shows that practically nothing could be done to turn these casks into a significant public hazard. Moreover, despite claims to the contrary, there appears to be no credible way in which an airplane could penetrate the reinforced, steel-lined, 1.5 m thick concrete walls surrounding a nuclear reactor. Evidence from the 1979 Three Mile Island and the 1986 Chernobyl incidents indicates that even in the event of a reactor breach, there would be few long-term effects on human health. Telling people that they (and the planet) are in grave danger from events that cannot cause significant harm plays into the hands of terrorists by fostering panic, the authors conclude.

Food Fears. Daniel Dupont. *Scientific American*, v. 289 pp20+ October 2003.

According to Dupont, agro-terrorism—the deliberate introduction of pathogens to sicken and destroy farm animals and crops—could inflict great damage on the nation's economy and food supply. A simulation exercise called Silent Prairie showed that contagious diseases could spread with alarming rapidity in food grains, cattle, and poultry, all of which are cultivated in close quarters. The author calls on the federal government to pay more attention to the threat.

Technology Can't Tame Terror. Erica Jonietz. *Technology Review*, v. 106 pp76–78 September 2003.

In an interview, the consultant Isaac Yeffet, former head of security for El Al Airlines, discusses how security could be tightened in American airports and how data-mining could be used to identify suspect passengers. Yeffet believes that technology is only as good as the people who apply it, and that airline personnel need thorough training, focused on terrorism rather than irrelevant offenses such as drunk driving or tax evasion, so that heightened security will not result in long delays, unnecessary breaches of privacy, or missed signals.

How Soccer Moms Became Security Moms. Joe Klein. *Time*, v. 161 pp23 February 17, 2003.

According to Klein, women's priority in the war on terrorism is protection of the home against the next terrorist attack. This concern is practical, defensive, and not as exciting as bombing an Al Qaeda leader. Dubbed homeland security, it has the added drawback of inspiring feelings of complete helplessness, Klein says. Almost half the American women respondents in a Gallup Organization October poll claim to believe they or a family member will soon be victims of an attack, but the polls do not describe the intensity of this worry.

The State of Our Defense. Romesh Ratnesar. *Time*, v. 161 pp24–29 February 24, 2003.

Ratnesar writes that, although the Bush administration believes Al Qaeda is ready to attack the United States again, questions arise regarding the efficacy of measures to improve homeland security. FBI fears of a devastating attack are as high as they have been in months, partly because of the possible involvement of biological and chemical weapons, but the United States still does not have a credible and comprehensive system established to deal with such attacks, Ratnesar says. Interviews with dozens of homeland security officials nationwide reveal that local authorities are more aware of the possibility of terrorist attacks but have insufficient resources to strengthen their defenses against them. Gaps in homeland security are being attributed to a lack of money, with experts from both parties agreeing that in this case increased funding would lead to more protection. Ratnesar concludes that there probably is no way of knowing whether the country is prepared for the next attack until after it occurs.

Will We Be Safer? Richard Lacayo et al. *Time*, v. 162 pp56–9 September 8, 2003.

Scientists are likely to come up with bold innovations to cope with terrorist threats, the authors write. Two years after the September 11 terrorist attacks, America is still worried about terrorism. According to the authors, there will be many, many Los Alamos–type projects spearheaded by various teams of researchers and engineers aiming to head off a mind-numbing range of potential threats. The writers discuss a number of these developments in three key areas: airports, bioterrorism, and port security.

Foreign Scholars in Visa Limbo. Charles W. Petit. *U.S. News & World Report,* v. 135 pp49 October 13, 2003.

The author reports that thousands of foreign students and scholars are waiting weeks or months for visas that were formerly routine. The majority of these are students in high-tech and science fields on the State Department's "technology alert list," which requires additional consular scrutiny and review by other agencies before a foreign student or researcher in a sensitive area is allowed to proceed. The resulting delays and confusion have impacted universities. America's higher education system, a crucial spur to the country's economic vigor, relies heavily on foreign students and staff, reports Petit. In addition to foreign faculty and visiting scholars, almost 600,000 international students are on 4,500-plus campuses.

FBI Curbed in Tracking Gun Buyers. Dan Eggen. *Washington Post*, pA1 November 18, 2003.

Eggen writes that the Justice Department's interpretation of the Brady bill prevents the FBI from investigating any legal gun purchase, even when the purchaser's name appears on the Bureau's Watch List of suspected terrorists and their sympathizers. (Sales that have been blocked by the provisions of the Brady law are open to investigation, however.) Eggen's sources suggest that more than a dozen people on the Watch List have attempted to purchase firearms in the past six months but cannot say how many have succeeded. The article includes comments by congressmen, Justice Department officials, FBI agents, and a spokesman for the National Rifle Association.

U.S. Set to Revise How It Tracks Some Visitors. Dan Eggen. *Washington Post*, pA1 November 21, 2003.

The Department of Homeland Security is considering ending the controversial visitor-registration program aimed primarily at men from Muslim countries. The program was started, and largely carried out, by the Justice Department; it became controversial when nearly 14,000 of the 83,000 voluntary registrants were detained and scheduled for deportation proceedings, sending shock waves through immigrant communities and provoking protests at home and abroad. An unknown number of people who had not yet registered then decided not to, thus making themselves illegal immigrants, while others concluded that America was no longer friendly and returned to their homelands or sought refuge in Canada. The Department of Homeland Security, which inherited the program when it took over immigration services, says that it has been a disappointment and that results do not justify its continuation.

Better Safe Than Sorry. Amitai Etzioni. *Weekly Standard*, v. 8 pp29–33 July 21, 2003.

Etzioni discusses the provisions of the Homeland Security bill and the opposition it has encountered in various sectors of American society. He argues that, by and large, new safety measures enacted in the wake of 9/11 are not encroachments on liberty but have a sound legal and ethical basis, as well as practical value. Some of the changes now under way were long overdue, while several others are also quite reasonable; only a few raise disturbing questions, he contends.

The Unwatched Ships at Sea: The Coast Guard and Homeland Security. H. D. S. Greenway. *World Policy Journal,* v. 20 pp73-8 Summer 2003.

In the wake of 9/11, Greenway says, the newest fear is that the country could be attacked through its seaports as well as from the air. The responsibility of protecting U.S. ports and the country's coastline falls to the Coast Guard, which heretofore has been undermanned, underfinanced, and ill-equipped. In an era of asymmetrical warfare, the Coast Guard has arguably become more important to the country's security than the Navy. On March 1, 2003, the Coast Guard service was incorporated into the Department of Homeland Security. Greenway highlights the Coast Guard's new responsibilities and discusses arguments over whether the Guard should be stripped of its ancillary missions in order to concentrate on preventing seaborne terrorism, or whether its overall capacity should be strengthened so that it can perform both old and new duties.

Index